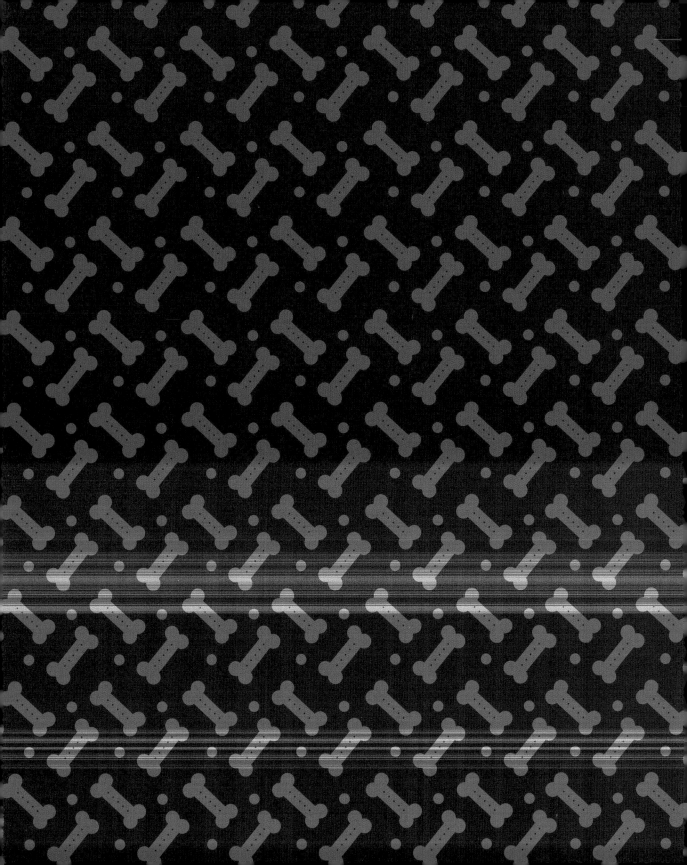

FOR ALL THE UNSUNG HEROES OF THE CANINE WORLD.

Text copyright © 2020 by Kimberlie Hamilton
Illustrations copyright © 2020 by Allie Runnion, Andrew Gardner, Becky Davies,
Charlotte Archer, Emma Jayne, Holly Sterling, Hui Skipp, Jessica Smith,
Katie Wilson, Lily Rossiter, Michelle Hird, Nan Lawson, Olivia Holden,
Rachel Allsop, Rachel Sanson, Bonnie Pang, and Sam Loman

Library of Congress Cataloging-in-Publication Data available

ISBN 978-1-338-61803-7

10 9 8 7 6 5 4 3 2 1   20 21 22 23 24

Printed in Malaysia   108
First printing June 2020

•DARING DOGS•

30

TRUE TALES OF

HEROIC HOUNDS

KIMBERLIE HAMILTON

ILLUSTRATIONS BY

ALLIE RUNNION, ANDREW GARDNER, BECKY DAVIES, CHARLOTTE ARCHER, EMMA JAYNE, HOLLY STERLING, HUI SKIPP, JESSICA SMITH, KATIE WILSON, LILY ROSSITER, MICHELLE HIRD, NAN LAWSON, OLIVIA HOLDEN, RACHEL ALLSOP, RACHEL SANSON, BONNIE PANG, AND SAM LOMAN

SCHOLASTIC PRESS / NEW YORK

CONTENTS

EAT. PLAY. LOVE.

The one-of-a-kind friendship between dogs and humans goes way, way, WAY back. As far back as tens of thousands of years!

In that time, dogs have done some truly amazing things with their lives. They have also earned a reputation for being loyal and loving, talented and trustworthy, with unique personalities and characteristics all their own.

This book will introduce you to more than thirty remarkable real-life canines from around the world and across the centuries. They have traveled into space, averted disasters, made great discoveries, and risked their own lives to save others.

These heroes with fur should be celebrated and remembered for many dog years to come. So, are you ready?

SIT...

STAY...

READ...

WHAT HAPPENED WHEN

14,000 BC
EARLIEST KNOWN DOG IS DISCOVERED IN GERMANY.

7000 BC
DOGS HEAD TO THE AMERICAS VIA A SIBERIAN LAND BRIDGE. BRRR!

2637 BC
DOGS SCORE A SPOT IN THE CHINESE ZODIAC (CATS DO NOT).

AD 300
PAMPERED PEKINGESE IN CHINA HAVE THEIR OWN SERVANTS.

LATE 1500s
CHARLES IX, KING OF FRANCE, DECLARES A DAY OF MOURNING AFTER HIS DOG DIES.

1884
GERMANY ESTABLISHES THE WORLD'S FIRST WAR DOG SCHOOL.

9000 BC
DOGS APPEAR IN EGYPTIAN TOMB ART.

1873
THE KENNEL CLUB IS FOUNDED IN BRITAIN TO SHOWCASE PUREBREDS.

C. 12,000 BC
FIRST HUMAN FOUND BURIED WITH HIS PET POOCH. AWWW!

C. 450 BC
PLATO SAYS, "A DOG HAS THE SOUL OF A PHILOSOPHER."

1890s
PARIS BECOMES FAMOUS FOR CANINE HAUTE COUTURE. OH LA LA!

1280
MONGOL LEADER (AND MEGA DOG LOVER) KUBLAI KHAN OWNS 5,000 MASTIFFS.

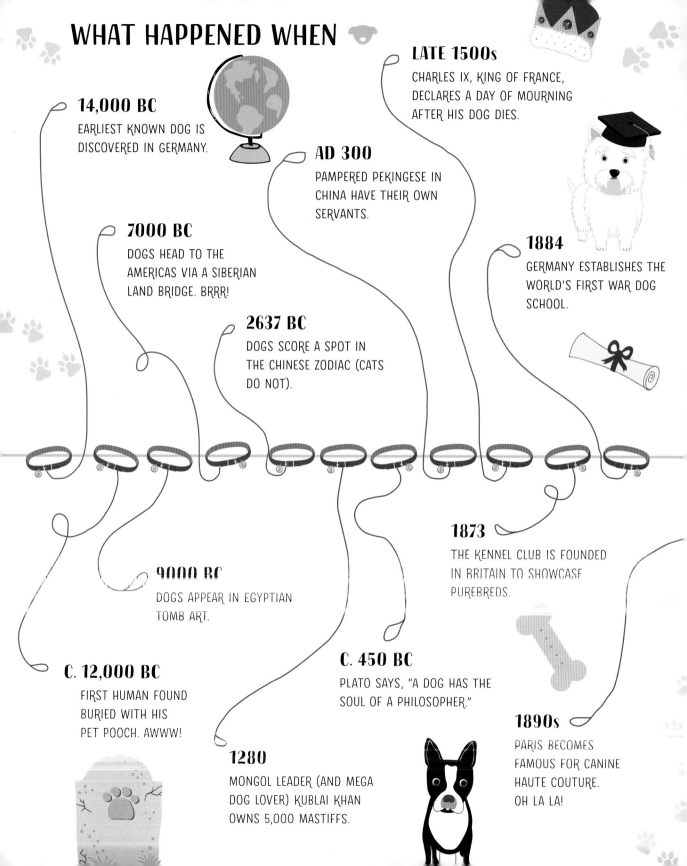

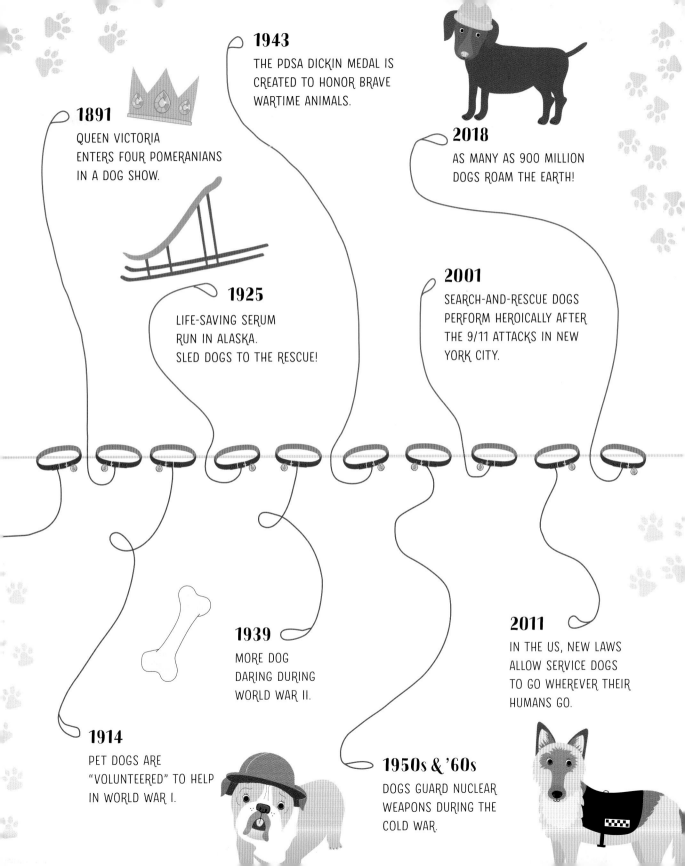

1891
QUEEN VICTORIA ENTERS FOUR POMERANIANS IN A DOG SHOW.

1943
THE PDSA DICKIN MEDAL IS CREATED TO HONOR BRAVE WARTIME ANIMALS.

2018
AS MANY AS 900 MILLION DOGS ROAM THE EARTH!

1925
LIFE-SAVING SERUM RUN IN ALASKA. SLED DOGS TO THE RESCUE!

2001
SEARCH-AND-RESCUE DOGS PERFORM HEROICALLY AFTER THE 9/11 ATTACKS IN NEW YORK CITY.

1939
MORE DOG DARING DURING WORLD WAR II.

2011
IN THE US, NEW LAWS ALLOW SERVICE DOGS TO GO WHEREVER THEIR HUMANS GO.

1914
PET DOGS ARE "VOLUNTEERED" TO HELP IN WORLD WAR I.

1950s & '60s
DOGS GUARD NUCLEAR WEAPONS DURING THE COLD WAR.

DARING DOGS!

ANTIS
THE DOG WHO COULD FLY

During World War II, Czech pilot Robert Bozdech was flying a mission over France when he was shot down by an enemy plane. He survived the crash and took shelter in a nearby farmhouse, empty save for a German shepherd puppy. After Robert was rescued, he took the puppy back to his air force base in England. He named the dog Antis and they became inseparable.

Antis soon proved himself to be a hero in his own right. After a nearby city was bombed, he raced to a collapsed building and began to sniff and paw through the rubble. Antis wasn't trained for rescue work but still managed to find six survivors. Robert had to carry an exhausted Antis back to base, his paws torn and bleeding.

Antis went missing once, right before Robert was due to fly out on a big mission. Robert and his crew were climbing to an altitude of nearly 6,000 feet when they were startled to see Antis, gasping for air in the thin atmosphere.

Robert ripped off his oxygen mask and put it over the stowaway's muzzle, alternating breaths with him for the entire flight. Despite heavy enemy fire and a bad storm, the crew survived and decided that Antis had brought them luck. Antis later took to the skies about thirty more times wearing a custom-made oxygen mask.

Robert took Antis home to Czechoslovakia (now known as the Czech Republic) when the war ended, but was forced to flee when another war broke out several years later. Antis helped Robert to navigate a number of dangerous border crossings, sniffing out the enemy and guiding him to freedom back in England. He was the first non-British dog to be awarded the PDSA Dickin Medal for brave wartime animals.

1939–1953
FRANCE / ENGLAND

THEY ALSO SERVED

During World War II, a special award was created for heroic animals like **ANTIS** who showed great bravery during wartime. Here are just a few who received the PDSA Dickin Medal:

The first canine recipient, **BOB**, saved his unit from capture in North Africa during World War II. On patrol one night, his white fur disguised with paint, Bob sensed the enemy hiding in the dark and led British soldiers to safety.

BRIAN was a collie mix para-dog who parachuted behind enemy lines on D-Day in 1944. **ROB**, another paratrooper collie, made more than twenty jumps!

English springer spaniel **BUSTER** was a bomb dog during the Iraq War in 2003. He was credited with saving the lives of a thousand British soldiers after finding a cache of weapons.

CHIPS served with the US Army and was the most decorated dog of World War II. He once charged a machine-gun nest, attacking enemy soldiers and forcing them to surrender.

A Newfoundland named **GANDER** is the only Canadian dog to ever win the Dickin Medal. He saved lives during the Battle of Hong Kong in 1941 and was killed in action while gathering a grenade.

GUNNER was an Australian kelpie who served as a remarkably reliable air-raid early warning system during World War II in Darwin, Australia.

A border collie in Scotland, **SHEILA**, was the first civilian dog to earn the Dickin Medal. She led a search party to find four American airmen lost in a blizzard after their plane crashed in 1944.

THE MAGNIFICENT SEVEN

Seven dogs earned the PDSA Dickin Medal for their efforts during the London Blitz of 1940:

- **BEAUTY**, A FOX TERRIER, INSPIRED A SPECIAL SQUAD TO LOCATE AND RESCUE TRAPPED ANIMALS.

- **IRMA** WAS A GERMAN SHEPHERD WHO FOUND 233 PEOPLE UNDER THE RUBBLE, INCLUDING TWENTY-ONE SURVIVORS.

- **JET** WAS A GERMAN SHEPHERD WHO REPORTED FOR DUTY EVERY SINGLE NIGHT OF THE BLITZ.

- **PETER**, A COLLIE MIX, FOUND VICTIMS UNDER BUILDINGS AND ONCE SAVED THE LIFE OF A SMALL BOY.

- **REX** WAS A DETERMINED GERMAN SHEPHERD UNDAUNTED BY SMOKE AND FLAMES.

- **RIP**, A FORMER STRAY, LOCATED MORE THAN ONE HUNDRED AIR-RAID VICTIMS.

- **THORN** WAS KNOWN FOR FEARLESSLY DASHING INTO BLAZING BUILDINGS TO SAVE PEOPLE TRAPPED INSIDE.

DID YOU KNOW?
THE PDSA DICKIN MEDAL—INSCRIBED WITH THE WORDS *FOR GALLANTRY* AND *WE ALSO SERVE*—HAS BEEN AWARDED SEVENTY-ONE TIMES SINCE 1943.

ARTHUR
AMAZON ADVENTURER

Adventure racing is a brutal test of endurance, with four-person teams running, cycling, and kayaking hundreds of miles in some of the toughest places on Earth. Racers must endure extreme temperatures, exhaustion, and lack of sleep, all while staying within 328 feet of their teammates.

At the 2014 World Championships, the Swedish team was midway through a grueling 430-mile race in the Amazon jungle. They had stopped for a meal break when team member Mikael Lindnord noticed a scruffy stray dog lurking nearby. Mikael tossed him a few meatballs and the dog wolfed them down.

Later, as the team struggled along slippery jungle trails, they realized the dog was following them. He kept up as they slogged through knee-deep mud and across swollen rivers. The dog seemed determined to join them, so they named him Arthur, in honor of Sweden's king.

The final stage of the race was a fourteen-hour sufferfest through treacherous swamps. It would be absurd to have a dog slowing them down. But as they pulled away from shore, they saw Arthur paddling toward them. Mikael hauled him into his kayak and the team carried on, finishing in twelfth place.

Mikael couldn't bear to leave Arthur behind, so he took him back to Sweden. Arthur has fully embraced life in his new home, romping in snow and swimming in icy lakes. But he hasn't entirely forgotten the hardships of his past life as a stray. He buries any leftovers in his food bowl, just to make sure he never goes hungry again.

BORN C. 2012
ECUADOR / SWEDEN

TRAILBLAZERS WITH TAILS

Dogs like **ARTHUR** have a nose for adventure. Here are some others who left their paw prints on new frontiers:

BOTHIE is the only dog to visit both the North and South Poles. The Jack Russell terrier was part of a three-year, around-the-world expedition that started in 1979. Dogs are no longer allowed in Antarctica, so his Guinness World Record will stand forever.

BUD was the first dog to cross America by automobile in 1903. The bull terrier and his human sidekick made the sixty-three-day journey in a car with no windshield or roof, so Bud wore goggles to keep the bugs and dust out of his eyes. What a sight that must have been!

GOBI crossed paths with an ultramarathon runner during a 155-mile race across China's Gobi Desert. The man named the pup Gobi after she stayed with him every step of the way, sharing his limited food and water. He lost the race but gained a forever friend.

LEONCICO was a yellow mutt who accompanied Spanish explorer and conquistador Vasco Núñez de Balboa across the steamy Isthmus of Panama in 1513. He was strong and fierce and strutted around in a gold collar bestowed upon him by his master.

OWNEY was abandoned as a puppy outside a New York State post office in 1888. He started following the mail bags, accompanying them across the United States and overseas by wagon, train, and steamship. No train he ever rode on was in an accident, making him a postal legend.

RED DOG gained fame for traveling around the Australian outback in the 1970s. The friendly Australian kelpie often hitched rides with strangers, happy to go wherever they were going. One time, when a newbie bus driver refused to let him onboard, all the passengers got off in protest.

RUPEE was rescued from the streets of India and became the first dog to reach Mount Everest Base Camp in the Himalayas. He and a team of climbers endured storms, mudslides, and a yak attack (!) before reaching base camp, where Rupee saw snow for the first time.

SEAMAN was part of the Lewis and Clark Expedition that mapped an unexplored part of America from 1804 to 1806. It was a risky journey and the black Newfoundland was credited with saving lives. He once chased off a buffalo that would have trampled the group as they slept.

ASHLEY WHIPPET
PHENOMENAL FRISBEE DOG

When Alex Stein first brought Ashley home as a three-week-old pup, he used an upside-down Frisbee as a makeshift dog bowl. The plastic disc became Ashley's favorite toy, and he and Alex played with it on the beach for hours. Crowds gathered to watch the dog sprint, spin, and spring high into the air.

Alex dreamed of a future in show business for his talented dog, but he never got far with that. Then Alex had an idea. An out-of-the-blue WILD idea.

It was the summer of 1974 and the Los Angeles Dodgers were hosting a nationally televised baseball game. Alex smuggled Ashley into the stadium, then ran onto the field between innings and hurled him a Frisbee. The crowd gasped as Ashley snatched the flying disc out of the air with a spectacular all-four-paws-off-the-ground leap.

Alex threw again and again as fifty thousand people cheered in the stands and millions more watched on TV. It was the debut of what would become a worldwide phenomenon known as dog Frisbee. The duo went on to perform on *The Tonight Show,* at the White House, and even during halftime at the Super Bowl. *Sports Illustrated* dubbed the super sleek athlete the "surest jaws on four paws."

After the World Frisbee Championships introduced a new canine division, Ashley won the title three years in a row. In one record-setting sprint, he ran 318 feet to make a catch! He so dominated the sport that the contest changed its name to the Ashley Whippet Invitational. His athletic legacy lives on to this day.

C. 1971–1985
COLUMBUS, OH

DOGSPOTTING FOR BEGINNERS

ASHLEY WHIPPET launched a worldwide sports phenomenon. Today there's an equally popular dog-related "sport" on social media: **DOGSPOTTING**.

DOGSPOTTING started off as a Facebook group for posting photos (or "spots") of dogs. It's easy to play—simply snap a photo of a random dog (one you don't know), post it, and score points based on twelve rules. It's all rather silly, but that's what makes it fun.

THE RULES ARE WHAT MAKE THE GAME CHALLENGING. They include things like: no photos of service dogs; no pictures of owners without permission; no selfies; and no "low-hanging fruit," such as spots taken at vet surgeries or dog parks (too easy!). **IT'S ALL ABOUT EMBRACING THE UNEXPECTED.**

EACH TIME YOU SPOT A DOG, ASK YOURSELF FOUR QUESTIONS:

1. DO YOU KNOW THE DOG? IF THE ANSWER IS YES, SKIP IT AND LOOK ELSEWHERE.

2. HOW BIG IS THE DOG? SIZE PROVIDES THE BASE SCORE FOR EVERY SPOT.

3. WHAT'S THE DOG DOING? DEPENDING ON THE ANSWER, YOU CAN EARN OR LOSE POINTS.

4.   IS THE DOG ALONE OR WITH OTHERS? "MULTI-SPOTS" ARE WORTH EXTRA POINTS.

BONUS POINTS
This is where things really get fun. Look for things like:

- **BRANCH MANAGER** — A DOG CARRYING A STICK **(2 POINTS)**
- **ACTION DOG** — ANY DOG PERFORMING ATHLETIC FEATS **(2 POINTS)**
- **CONE OF SHAME** — A DOG WEARING A CONE **(3 POINTS)**
- **RONIN** — A DOG WITHOUT A MASTER, CARRYING ITS OWN LEASH **(4 POINTS)**
- **HERO DOG** — A DOG PERFORMING A HEROIC ACT OF SOME KIND **(25 POINTS)**

Some spots can actually cost you points, like a "reverse spot"—that's when a dog catches you looking at him! Points are also deducted for things like **SHAMEFUL TRANSPORT** (like a dog in a stroller or handbag) or **SHAMEFUL APPEARANCE** (any dog dressed in an embarrassing manner).

Not into social media? No worries! You can enjoy **DOGSPOTTING** by yourself or with friends, just by taking photos or keeping track of spots in a notebook. You can even make up your own rules and scoring system!

BOBBIE
CROSS-COUNTRY TREKKER

During a family vacation far from home, a friendly collie mix named **BOBBIE** somehow became lost. His heartbroken family returned home to Silverton, Oregon, without him, never expecting to see their beloved pet again.

Six months later, Bobbie was spotted on the streets of Silverton. He was dirty and scrawny and the pads of his paws were worn down to next to nothing. It is estimated that he had walked as far as 3,000 miles, crossing rivers and plains, deserts and mountains to get back to his family.

How did he do it? After the story appeared in national newspapers, people who had looked after Bobbie the Wonder Dog along his journey wrote to his family. Their stories helped piece together his epic cross-country route.

Bobbie had more or less retraced the exact route that his family had taken. He met many kindhearted strangers who gave him food or medical care or a safe place to rest. If only Bobbie could talk! He'd have some stories to tell, for sure.

Bobbie's against-all-odds saga inspired pet parades, memorials, murals, books, and films (including a silent film, *The Call of the West*, starring Bobbie as himself). Fan letters poured in from around the world and he was presented with a jewel-studded collar and the keys to various cities.

Bobbie was buried at the Oregon Humane Society pet cemetery in Portland, and canine film star Rin Tin Tin laid a wreath at his grave. The town of Silverton still celebrates Bobbie Day each year on February 15, the anniversary of the date he finally returned home.

1921–1927
SILVERTON, OR

DROOLWORTHY DESTINATIONS

Most dogs will never travel as far as Bobbie, either by chance or by choice. But if they could choose to take a trip, here are some places they might go:

At the annual **AMERICAN KENNEL CLUB NATIONAL AGILITY CHAMPIONSHIP** in the United States, dogs navigate complex obstacle courses featuring tunnels, seesaws, poles, and bridges.

Dogs and humans work in sync at the **NATIONAL SHEEPDOG TRIAL CHAMPIONSHIPS** in Australia, herding sheep through a tricky course and into a pen. It's all done with whistled commands!

Water-loving dogs head to **DOCKDOGS** events across the United States, vying to jump the farthest, fastest, and highest off the end of a dock. The Iron Dog champ excels in all three categories.

The **GOLDEN RETRIEVER FESTIVAL** in Scotland is celebrated at the breed's ancestral home. More than 200 dogs gather on the grounds, making for a "golden" photo opportunity.

At the **TOMPKINS SQUARE PARK HALLOWEEN DOG PARADE** in New York City, pets dressed in creative getups (like Harry Potter and Tinker Bell) compete to win prizes for Best in Show.

The **IDITAROD**, the world's toughest dogsled race, is held every March in Alaska. It stretches more than one hundred miles from Anchorage to Nome and takes about nine days.

During the Hindu festival of Diwali in Nepal, **KUKUR TIHAR** is a day devoted to honoring dogs. They are adorned with floral garlands and red tikkas on their foreheads, and served delicious food.

The Palme d'Or is the top prize awarded at the glamorous Cannes Film Festival in France. But there's also the **PALM DOG AWARD** for the best performance by a dog (live or animated).

Bolivia celebrates **SAINT ROCH'S DAY** every August 16 with parades of costumed dogs. Saint Roch is the Catholic patron saint of dogs, and legend has it that a dog once saved his life.

The **SURF CITY SURF DOG** competition in Huntington Beach, California, attracts wave-riding, adrenaline-junkie hounds from across the country, all hoping to win the coveted Surf Dog title.

Purebred dogs at the **WESTMINSTER KENNEL CLUB DOG SHOW** in New York City dream of being named Best of Breed, Best of Group, and—for ultimate bragging rights—Best in Show.

Popular events at the annual **WOOFSTOCK** in Toronto, Canada, include dog speed dating, tricks, Mr. and Ms. Canine Canada, and the not-to-be-missed Running of the Pugs.

BRANDY
DISASTER-AVERTING BOMB DOG

On a perfectly ordinary day in 1972, an anonymous caller demanded $2 million or he'd blow up an airplane. Every jet at New York's John F. Kennedy International Airport was immediately grounded. Planes in the air were told to land ASAP.

Flight 7, en route from New York to Los Angeles, turned back and its passengers and crew were rushed off the plane. The clock was ticking and the bomb was set to go off in just a few hours. The plane was searched, yet nothing was found. Bomb experts feared they missed something.

By sheer chance, a New York Police Department dog named Brandy was at the airport that day. Airports didn't have bomb-sniffing dogs back then, and the German shepherd was there only to do a demonstration of her skills. Instead, she was called upon to perform in a real life-or-death emergency.

Brandy trotted onto the plane and swiftly honed in on a briefcase marked CREW in the cockpit. Then she did what she was trained to do—she sat down to signal she'd found something. The bomb squad looked skeptical. Nothing about the briefcase seemed suspicious—it looked like a case that typically held flight manuals. But Brandy refused to budge.

The bomb experts gingerly opened the case. Inside, they found enough of a powerful explosive to destroy the plane. The bomb was whisked away and disarmed minutes before it was set to explode. Phew!

It was the first time a bona fide bomb had been found onboard a US airline. Thanks to Brandy, bomb-sniffing dogs now work at all major airports and the skies are much safer because of it.

C. 1970–UNKNOWN
QUEENS, NY

SCENT-SATIONAL SNIFFERS

If a human can smell a teaspoon of sugar in a cup of coffee, a dog like **BRANDY** can smell a teaspoon of sugar in a million gallons of water. That's nearly enough to fill two Olympic-sized swimming pools! Here are some more good-to-nose facts about **SNIFFER DOGS**:

- DOGS CAN BE TRAINED TO DETECT ALL SORTS OF THINGS, INCLUDING DRUGS, WEAPONS, EXPLOSIVES, STOLEN GOODS, AND BLOOD. EVEN BEDBUGS. (EWWW!)

- HUMANS HAVE TRIED BUT STILL HAVEN'T COME UP WITH TECHNOLOGY THAT CAN OUT-SNIFF A DOG.

- BOMB-DETECTION DOGS ARE TRAINED TO SIT ONCE THEY'VE FOUND WHAT THEY'RE LOOKING FOR. WHY? NO ONE WANTS A DOG PAWING AND SCRATCHING AT SOMETHING THAT COULD BLOW THEM SKY-HIGH.

- ELEPHANTS AND RODENTS SMELL AT LEAST AS WELL AS DOGS, BUT DOGS ACE THE COMPETITION IN TERMS OF ATTITUDE. NO OTHER ANIMAL IS SO EAGER TO PLEASE OR DO WHAT HUMANS ASK OF IT

- SOME OF THE BEST BOMB DETECTORS ARE GERMAN SHEPHERDS AND LABRADOR RETRIEVERS. SHEPHERDS ARE "PLAY REWARD" DOGS THAT WILL WORK HARD ALL DAY JUST SO SOMEONE WILL TOSS A BALL FOR THEM. LABRADORS ARE CONSTANTLY HUNGRY AND THUS ARE "FOOD REWARD" DOGS.

🐾 A BOMB-DETECTION DOG DOESN'T SMELL A BOMB SO MUCH AS THE CHEMICALS USED TO MAKE IT. IF A BOMB WAS A PIZZA, A DOG WOULDN'T THINK, "I SMELL PIZZA!" HE'D THINK, "I SMELL TOMATOES, GARLIC, AND CHEESE." SO, A BOMB DETECTION DOG IS LOOKING FOR THE CHEESE ON THE PIZZA, NOT THE PIZZA!

SNIFFER DOG HALL OF FAME

DAKOTA was a pit bull who helped with more than one hundred searches, including recovery efforts for the astronauts who lost their lives in the 2003 Space Shuttle *Columbia* tragedy.

Some sniffer dogs can detect cancerous cells. One of the best was **GEORGE**, a schnauzer with a 99 percent success rate. He was so good that he was featured on TV's *Unsolved Mysteries*.

MEGAN made one hundred finds over the course of her seven-year career at England's Gatwick Airport. The record-breaking springer spaniel found 485 pounds of cocaine worth about $38 million!

After a series of bombings in Mumbai, India, in 1993, a Labrador retriever named **ZANJEER** saved thousands of lives by locating other explosives, detonators, and live ammunition.

BUDDY
AMERICA'S FIRST SEEING EYE DOG

Before there were guide dogs in the United States, blind people had to depend on others for pretty much everything. But all of that changed thanks to a dog named Buddy.

In 1927, a popular magazine published an article about a program in Europe that trained dogs to be guides for war-blinded soldiers. The father of nineteen-year-old Morris Frank wrote to the author—an American dog breeder and trainer living in Switzerland, Dorothy Harrison Eustis—and begged her to help his son, who had lost sight in both eyes.

The woman invited Morris to come and meet her and introduced him to a beautiful and keenly intelligent German shepherd. Morris called her Buddy, and they spent several months learning how to work together, communicating through the stiff handle of her harness.

When Morris returned to New York City, a throng of journalists eagerly waited to see America's first guide dog in action. One reporter dared them to cross a street jammed with taxis and people and buses. It was a bigger challenge than anything Morris and Buddy had ever faced in training, but she calmly navigated the traffic like a champ.

Morris went on to establish the Seeing Eye, the first guide dog school in the United States. With Buddy at his side, he fought to change laws so that visually impaired people would be allowed to go anywhere with their dogs, including restaurants, workplaces, and public transport.

Morris liked to say that Buddy had given him the "divine gift of freedom." She paved the way for thousands of other service dogs working today.

C. 1928–1938
SWITZERLAND / NEW YORK

HOUNDS WHO LOVE TO HELP

BUDDY was more than Morris Frank's best friend—she helped him regain his confidence and independence. These days, **SERVICE DOGS** (aka assistance dogs) help people in all kinds of ways.

GUIDE DOGS lead visually impaired people around obstacles. They've been assisting blind people for centuries, as far back as ancient Roman times!

HEARING DOGS help people who are deaf or hearing impaired, alerting them to noises such as alarms, doorbells, or crying babies.

MOBILITY ASSISTANCE DOGS—like the one belonging to former president George H. W. Bush, Sully—can open doors, retrieve items on command, and do all sorts of other everyday tasks. Sully even helped the late president cast a ballot in an election!

DIABETIC ALERT DOGS can detect chemical changes in blood sugar and either alert their human or sound an alarm if medical help is needed.

SEIZURE RESPONSE DOGS are trained to bark or to press an alarm if someone is having an epileptic seizure. They can also move the person to a safe place and fetch medicine or a phone.

PSYCHIATRIC SERVICE DOGS assist people dealing with emotional conditions like depression, anxiety, and post-traumatic stress disorder (PTSD).

AUTISM SUPPORT DOGS are a big help for kids on the spectrum. They act as an icebreaker in social situations and are a comforting friend in times of stress.

ALLERGY DETECTION DOGS are trained to sniff out allergens such as peanuts or gluten. They are often paired with children.

SERVICE DOG HALL OF FAME

ENDAL was a Labrador retriever who was the **MOST FAMOUS ASSISTANCE DOG** in the United Kingdom. He knew over a hundred voice commands and hand signals, could fetch items from shelves, load and empty a washing machine, and even get money out of an ATM. He was awarded a **PDSA GOLD MEDAL** and voted **SERVICE DOG OF THE MILLENNIUM**.

DID YOU KNOW? SERVICE DOGS ARE TRAINED TO TAKE A "NATURE BREAK" ON DEMAND!

CAESAR
COMPANION TO A KING

———————————⬭———————————

Caesar, a feisty fox terrier, was the loyal companion of Queen Victoria's eldest son, Edward VII. Caesar was a rather high-strung little thing but also the king's most cherished friend.

Caesar slept in a chair beside the king's bed and reclined next to his throne while important matters were discussed. He had his own footman to groom him and tend to his needs. An artist painted his portrait several times, and master jeweler Fabergé made a model of him studded with precious gems. Caesar even wore a collar with a tag that proudly proclaimed, "I am Caesar. I belong to the King." This was one royally pampered pet.

When the king passed away, Caesar was so depressed that he wouldn't eat and hid trembling under the royal bed. Queen Alexandra had never been too fond of Caesar, but seeing his grief changed her attitude. They had both lost someone very dear to them and took great comfort from each other.

As the king's funeral procession wound through the streets of London, thousands of people lined the route to pay their final respects. Caesar walked mournfully behind his master's coffin, a sight that tugged at the heartstrings of the British people. He was given a place of honor at the front of the procession, before heads of state and nine other kings. And rightly so.

Caesar's undying devotion was immortalized in a sculpture of the king and queen atop their tomb at Windsor Castle. Look closely and you'll see a stone likeness of Caesar at his royal companion's feet. Together for all eternity.

1898–1914
ENGLAND

ROYAL ROVERS

Edward VII was one of many blue bloods who loved dogs. A host of royal hounds have roamed the halls and grounds of palaces and castles throughout the ages, including breeds like these:

The **BICHON FRISE** is a little dog that's been a big hit with European royalty. Henry III of England loved his dogs so much that he carried them everywhere in a basket tied around his neck.

Henry VIII and other notable Tudors kept **GREYHOUNDS**, as did Queen Victoria's husband and Catherine the Great of Russia, who had her portrait painted with her favorite, Zemira.

KING CHARLES SPANIELS were named for Charles II, who was said to care more about his dogs than his kingdom. They were often used as foot warmers and flea magnets in royal beds!

The day Mary Queen of Scots was beheaded, she had her **MALTESE TERRIER** hidden under her skirt. The loyal dog refused to leave her mistress even after the grisly deed was done.

PEKINGESE were considered sacred in ancient China and worthy of a queen centuries later. One that was gifted to Queen Victoria—Looty—enjoyed a life of luxury at Windsor Castle.

Queen Elizabeth II has owned more than thirty **PEMBROKE WELSH CORGIS**, sometimes a dozen at a time. Princess Diana referred to them as "the moving carpet."

Queen Victoria bred **POMERANIANS** and entered them into dog shows. At one point, she had thirty-five. Luckily, Buckingham Palace offered plenty of room for her huge menagerie of pets!

Louis XIV of France adored toy **POODLES** and gave them the run of the Palace of Versailles. He had one pooch that he especially doted on, Filou, which means "trickster" in French.

Known for their elegance, stamina, and speed, **SALUKIS** were highly regarded by the ancient Egyptians. Even the boy king Tutankhamen was a saluki fan.

SHIH TZUS were prized in ancient China for their lionlike features. They were bred as gifts for the emperors, and anybody found with one outside the imperial court was sentenced to death.

DID YOU KNOW?
GREAT BRITAIN'S DUKE AND DUCHESS OF CAMBRIDGE, WILLIAM AND KATE, HAVE A COCKER SPANIEL. THE DUKE AND DUCHESS OF SUSSEX, HARRY AND MEGHAN, ARE BIG DOG LOVERS, TOO. THEY HAVE A BEAGLE AND A BLACK LABRADOR.

FORTUNE
NAPOLEON'S PINT-SIZE NEMESIS

Before she married Napoleon Bonaparte, Marie-Josèphe-Rose de Beauharnais was imprisoned during the French Revolution just for being an aristocrat. She was forbidden to write letters but allowed visits from her cute pug, Fortune. Her clueless captors never suspected that she tucked notes under Fortune's velvet collar. He smuggled them out to her friends, right under the guards' noses.

Rose's friends pulled some strings to free her from prison, and soon after, she fell in love with the future emperor of France, Napoleon. He wasn't wild about her name, so he called her Joséphine instead. He wasn't wild about dogs, either, which became something of a problem. Quite a big problem, actually.

Fortune was used to having her mistress all to herself and became quite annoyed when others lingered too long in her company. This led to a rather awkward incident on Joséphine and Napoleon's wedding night when the groom entered the bridal chamber and found Fortune curled up in her usual spot on the bed.

Napoleon demanded (as generals tend to do) that the dog be removed at once. Joséphine assured him that her precious little Fortune wasn't going anywhere. He could share the bed with his new wife and her furry friend or he could sleep elsewhere.

Napoleon being Napoleon, he tried to remove the dog by force. Bad idea. Fortune's sharp little teeth sank into the general's flesh. Needless to say, this didn't endear Fortune or any other dog to Napoleon, and he bore a scar for the rest of his life.

C. 1794–UNKNOWN
FRANCE

YANKEE DOODLE DAWGS

FORTUNE wasn't the only dog to share living quarters with a powerful leader. In America, more than a hundred dogs have lived with presidents at the White House.

GEORGE W. BUSH had two Scottish terriers, **BARNEY** and **MISS BEAZLEY**, as well as an English springer spaniel named **SPOT**. Barney had his own website with Barney Cam videos, filmed with a camera hung around his neck.

BARACK OBAMA promised his daughters they could get a dog after the 2008 election, no matter who won. Portuguese water dog **BO** was the first to join the family, followed later by **SUNNY**.

BUDDY was a chocolate Labrador who belonged to **BILL CLINTON**. He didn't get along too well with Socks, the Clintons' cat, who eventually opted to go and live with the president's personal secretary.

FAITHFUL belonged to **ULYSSES S. GRANT'S SON**, who received the pony-sized Newfoundland after the loss of another much-loved pet. When Grant moved in with the pony-sized Newfoundland, he told the staff, "If this dog dies, every employee in the White House will be discharged at once." He meant it, too!

FRANKLIN DELANO ROOSEVELT had seven dogs, but the most famous was his Scottish terrier, **FALA**. When FDR died, Fala walked in his funeral procession and is the only dog to ever be included in a presidential memorial.

GERALD FORD'S golden retriever had an all-American name, **LIBERTY**. She gave birth to nine puppies while living at the White House.

MILLIE was an English springer spaniel who "authored" a bestselling 1992 memoir about life in the White House. **GEORGE H. W. BUSH** once said, "My dog Millie knows more about foreign affairs than those two bozos," referring to **AL GORE** and **BILL CLINTON**.

JOHN F. KENNEDY kept a number of dogs at the White House, including **PUSHINKA** (aka Fluff), an adorable mutt who was a gift from the Soviet Union. Fluff's mom was a famous space dog!

THEODORE ROOSEVELT had many dogs but his favorite was **ROLLO**, a Saint Bernard. Rollo was a gentle giant well-known for his love of children.

A mixed-breed dog named **YUKI** was **LYNDON B. JOHNSON'S** constant companion. They swam together, slept in the same bed, and even danced with each other at his daughter's wedding.

HACHIKO
FAMOUSLY FAITHFUL

Hachiko was an Akita who lived in Tokyo with a man named Professor Ueno. When the professor first saw him, he thought the dog's slightly crooked legs looked like the Japanese kanji for the number eight (八, pronounced "hachi"), so he named him Hachiko.

Hachiko walked the professor to the train station each morning, and every afternoon he never failed to be there when his friend returned. But one fateful day, the professor died at work and never came home again. Hachiko continued to wait for him as he always did. Day after day, he went to the station precisely at 3 p.m. and waited and waited, searching for his friend among the strangers passing by. And he kept on waiting, for nearly ten years.

Local residents came to know Hachiko's heartbreaking story and kindly looked after him. Newspaper articles were written about him, and his unwavering loyalty made him a legend in Japan. A well-known artist even made a bronze statue of him, which was placed in front of the station where Hachiko patiently sat each day.

Hachiko kept up his faithful vigil until the day he died, and he was laid to rest next to the professor in a Tokyo cemetery. His statue was melted down for the war effort in World War II, but a new one later replaced it, and it's now a popular meeting spot.

Books and films have been made about Hachiko's life, and his devotion continues to inspire people around the world. He is honored with a memorial service each year on the anniversary of his death on March 8.

1923–1935
JAPAN

FRIENDS FUR-EVER

Two-legged or four, good friends like **HACHIKO** stick by you no matter what!

CAPITAN slept on his master's grave in Argentina for more than a decade. Cemetery staff looked after the devoted German shepherd so that he never had to leave.

A German shepherd named **CONSTANTINE** was the sole survivor of a car crash that killed his entire human family in Russia. He returned to the crash site over and over for the next seven years.

FIDO was a mixed-breed dog in Italy whose master died in World War II. Fido ("faithful one" in Latin) waited for him to return for the next fourteen years. He became so famous for his loyalty that his death was announced with a front-page obituary.

Golden retriever **LADY** was the loyal companion of an elderly American who started to lose his memory. When the man went missing, police searched for a week before they found Lady in a field, guarding the body of her dead master.

RUSWARP was a border collie who disappeared while hiking with his owner in Wales. Eleven weeks later, the man's body was found, still guarded by his dog. Ruswarp was so weak he had to be carried off the mountain and lived just long enough to attend the man's funeral.

SHEP was a herding dog in Montana whose owner died in 1936. The man's family sent for his body and Shep followed the casket to the railway station and watched as it was taken away. He stayed at the station, waiting for his master to return, for the next five and a half years.

A German shepherd in Argentina, **TALERO**, stayed with his master for twenty-three days after the man died in a snowstorm. Talero apparently tried to keep his owner warm by laying on top of him.

PDSA Dickin Medal recipient **THEO** was an English springer spaniel whose best buddy was a British soldier. The man was killed in action in Afghanistan and Theo died just hours later, many said of a broken heart.

WAGHYA belonged to a king in India in 1680. When the king died, his body was cremated in the traditional Hindu way. According to legend, Waghya leaped onto the burning pyre to be with his master forever.

DID YOU KNOW?
GREYFRIARS BOBBY WAS A SKYE TERRIER IN EDINBURGH WHO SUPPOSEDLY SPENT EVERY NIGHT AT HIS MASTER'S GRAVE FOR FOURTEEN YEARS. WHETHER FACT OR FICTION, HIS STORY HAS MADE HIM A SCOTTISH FOLK HERO.

JOCK
THE BUSHVELD'S LEGENDARY HERO

Percy "Fitz" FitzPatrick set out in search of adventure and fortune in the late 1800s in the Bushveld region of South Africa. His gold rush dreams turned out to be a bust, so he bought a wagon and some oxen and started working as a transport rider.

Driving supplies around the region in those days was hot, lonely, back-breaking work. Many men got a dog to keep them company, go with them on hunting trips, and act as an extra set of eyes in the danger-fraught bush. When a friend's dog gave birth to some bull terrier mix puppies, Fitz adopted the runt of the litter and named him Jock.

This was the start of many shared adventures. One time, Jock and Fitz came upon an exhausted and terrified impala surrounded by a pack of wild dogs. Jock lunged at the vicious beasts, attacking again and again until they ran off. The impala took a few moments to compose herself before returning to the safety of her herd. She paused to look back at Jock, as if to say "Thank you!" for saving her life.

Fitz came to consider Jock far more valuable than any gold he might have discovered. His canine companion lived out his life at Fitz's side and inspired many bedtime stories for the man's children.

Fitz later shared these tales in *Jock of the Bushveld*, which became a bestseller and is now considered a South African classic. Movies have been made about Jock's life and statues created in his honor, and there are road markers along the Jock of the Bushveld Way, tracing the road the famous pair traveled.

1885–UNKNOWN
SOUTH AFRICA

INCREDIBLE (BUT TRUE) DOG FACTS

- PUPPIES ARE BORN DEAF, BLIND, AND TOOTHLESS BUT WITH A FULLY DEVELOPED SENSE OF SMELL.

- SOME DOGS ARE BORN ONE COLOR, BUT THEIR COAT PATTERNS CHANGE OVER TIME.

- DOGS FIND IT EASIER TO SEE A MOVING OBJECT THAN ONE THAT IS STANDING STILL.

- CHOCOLATE IS TOXIC TO DOGS. DITTO FOR GRAPES, RAISINS, AVOCADOS, AND COFFEE.

- SMALL BREEDS USUALLY LIVE LONGER THAN LARGE BREEDS. MUTTS USUALLY OUTLIVE PUREBREDS.

- THERE CAN BE ANYWHERE FROM ONE TO TWENTY-FOUR PUPPIES IN A SINGLE LITTER.

- THE MOST POPULAR BREED IN NORTH AMERICA AND GREAT BRITAIN IS THE LABRADOR RETRIEVER.

- IF YOU POINT AT SOMETHING, ONLY A DOG KNOWS TO LOOK IN THAT DIRECTION AND NOT AT YOUR ARM.

- MOST DOGS ENJOY PLAYDATES WITH OTHER DOGS BECAUSE THEIR ANCESTORS WERE PACK ANIMALS.

- OF THE 350 TO 400 KNOWN DOG BREEDS TODAY, 193 ARE RECOGNIZED BY THE AMERICAN KENNEL CLUB.

- IT COSTS ABOUT $60,000 TO TRAIN A NAVY SEAL DOG.

- WHEN DOGS FEEL STRESSED, THEIR PAWS GET MOIST, JUST LIKE HUMAN HANDS DO.

- WHEN DOGS POOP, THEY PREFER TO DO IT IN ALIGNMENT WITH THE EARTH'S MAGNETIC FIELD.

- STUDIES SHOW THAT DOGS HAVE A SENSE OF TIME AND MISS US WHEN WE'RE AWAY.

- IN CHINESE ASTROLOGY, PEOPLE BORN IN THE YEAR OF THE DOG ARE LOYAL AND HONEST.

- THE ANCIENT EGYPTIANS GAVE THEIR DOGS NAMES LIKE BLACKIE, RELIABLE, AND BRAVE ONE.

- THE UNITED STATES HAS THE HIGHEST DOG POPULATION IN THE WORLD. FRANCE HAS THE SECOND HIGHEST.

- THE AVERAGE DOG CAN RUN ABOUT NINETEEN MILES PER HOUR. GREYHOUNDS CAN RUN AT SPEEDS OF FORTY-FIVE MILES PER HOUR.

- PETTING A DOG HAS BEEN PROVEN TO LOWER BLOOD PRESSURE.

- DOGS ENJOY SWEET TASTES MUCH MORE THAN CATS DO.

- A DOG'S URINE CAN INDICATE THAT IT IS FEMALE OR MALE, OLD OR YOUNG, SICK OR HEALTHY, HAPPY OR ANGRY.

- A GERMAN COUNTESS LEFT $106 MILLION TO HER GERMAN SHEPHERD WHEN SHE DIED IN 1992.

- THE BASENJI IS THE ONLY BREED OF DOG THAT DOESN'T BARK (BUT IT CAN YODEL!).

- SURVEYS SAY THAT 33 PERCENT OF PET PARENTS TALK TO THEIR DOGS ON THE PHONE WHILE THEY ARE AWAY.

- BETWEEN 15 AND 30 PERCENT OF ALL DALMATIANS ARE DEAF IN ONE OR BOTH EARS.

JOFI
FREUD'S FURRY ASSISTANT

Sigmund Freud was the father of psychoanalysis, a dog lover, and a pioneer in canine-assisted therapy. His chow chow, Jofi, helped the famous doctor during sessions with his patients.

Freud believed that Jofi had a knack for sizing people up. If someone was relaxed, Jofi sat close enough to be patted. If someone was trying to hide their true feelings, Jofi moseyed across the room. Jofi also had a calming effect on patients, especially children, and everyone seemed to respond more openly and honestly whenever she was around.

During therapy sessions, Freud's patients reclined on a tapestry-draped couch as they shared their innermost thoughts. Jofi sprawled nearby and Freud often made comments as if from her point of view. If she wanted to be let out, Freud might remark, "Jofi doesn't approve of what you're saying." If she wanted back in, he'd say, "Jofi has decided to give you another chance." Once Jofi jumped up on an emotional patient, and Freud exclaimed, "Jofi is so excited that you've discovered the source of your anxiety!"

Jofi had another rare talent—she knew exactly when a one-hour therapy session was over. Whenever she got up and headed for the door, patients knew their time with Freud was up.

Did Freud ever wonder what went on inside Jofi's mind? No one knows for sure, although he was known to say, "Dogs love their friends and bite their enemies." He cherished Jofi for her love, her devotion, and her black-and-white perspective on life.

1930–1937
AUSTRIA

WORK LIKE A DOG!

With their dedication, devotion, and people-pleasing dispositions, dogs like **JOFI** make the best employees ever.

DUKE served as the mayor of a tiny town in Minnesota until he passed away in 2019. He won in an election in 2014—even his (human) opponent voted for him! Duke earned an annual salary paid in food, which for a Great Pyrenees is a LOT of kibble.

GABI was a German shepherd guard dog at the Belgrade Zoo in Serbia. She became famous in the late 1980s when she chased down a jaguar that had escaped its enclosure.

GRACIE is a **"BARK RANGER"** in Montana. Part of her job is herding bighorn sheep and mountain goats, keeping them away from Glacier National Park visitors. Perfect work for a border collie!

A Labrador truffle hunter in Oregon, **GUSTO** sniffs out fungi that is highly prized by chefs around the world. It's a job traditionally done by pigs, but dogs like Gusto are even better at it.

K9 KILLER tracks down poachers in Kruger National Park, South Africa. The Belgian Malinois earned a **PDSA GOLD MEDAL** for his efforts to save rhinos, which are hunted for their valuable horns.

LILA initially gained fame for her lobster-diving tricks, but now she's using her swimming skills to help clean up plastic bottles and other garbage polluting the ocean in Boca Raton, Florida.

American photographer William Wegman's top model was his Weimaraner, **MAN RAY**. Dressed in elaborate costumes, Man Ray's portraits were so famous that he was named **MAN OF THE YEAR** in 1982 by the *Village Voice* newspaper.

PIPER worked as a wildlife control officer at an airport in Michigan. Collisions with birds and other wildlife can be dangerous, so it was the border collie's job to keep runways clear.

Springer spaniel **ROSCOE** was a fire investigation dog in London who helped solve arson crimes and deterred would-be arsonists. He was named **ANIMAL OF THE YEAR** by the International Fund for Animal Welfare in 2016.

A German shepherd police dog in Colombia, South America, **SOMBRA**, is behind more than 245 arrests and the recovery of lots of illegal drugs. Bad guys put a bounty on her life, so she now has armed guards to protect her.

TILLAMOOK CHEDDAR was a Jack Russell terrier in New York City who created art using a touch-sensitive recording device. She had more than twenty solo shows in the United States and Europe.

JUDY
COURAGEOUS PRISONER OF WAR

Judy was an English pointer who served as a British Royal Navy mascot during World War II. She was onboard a vessel when it was bombed by enemy planes off Indonesia and everyone had to abandon ship.

The survivors were marooned on an island for days without food or water, until Judy discovered a freshwater spring that saved them. When the men were captured and driven to a camp for prisoners of war (POWs), they hid Judy and took her with them. At another POW camp, Judy met a half-starved airman named Frank Williams who shared his maggot-infested rice with her. From that moment on, he was her human.

Judy brought the prisoners fruit and rats to eat and alerted them to deadly snakes and scorpions. One time, she dragged an elephant's leg bone back to camp and spent hours digging a huge hole for it. The guards loathed her for trying to protect prisoners, and Frank feared for her life. He convinced the commander to register her as a POW, the only animal to ever be granted this status.

When the prisoners were herded onto a ship, Frank smuggled Judy onboard in a sack. But the ship was torpedoed, and Frank shoved her out a porthole in a desperate attempt to save her. Judy rescued many men herself that day, guiding them to floating debris and letting them hang on to her as she swam.

Judy's and Frank's ordeals weren't over yet, but he credited her with giving him a reason to live. The POWs were finally freed in 1945, and Frank took Judy home to England, where she was awarded the PDSA Dickin Medal.

1936–1950
INDONESIA / ENGLAND

KHAN
FOUR-LEGGED WAR HERO

Khan was a German shepherd who was volunteered for the British war effort in 1942, after his family heard a radio appeal for strong, intelligent dogs. Trained to find explosives, Khan was a star at the War Dog Training School and joined a battalion of the Scottish Rifles. Lance Corporal James Muldoon became his handler, a pairing that changed their lives forever.

Rifleman Khan and James formed a close bond right from the start. In 1944, they were part of a daring mission to liberate a Dutch island from the Nazis. Their boat came under heavy fire and collapsed, tipping the soldiers into thick mud and icy water. Khan fought his way to shore and immediately started looking for James, who was still in the water.

James didn't know how to swim and was sinking under the weight of his heavy pack. By some miracle, Khan heard his call for help over the deafening chaos of combat. He plunged back into the surf, swimming 200 yards to rescue his friend. He seized the soldier by his collar and pulled him to shore, then collapsed from exhaustion.

After the war, Khan was awarded the PDSA Dickin Medal and returned home to his family, despite James's appeals to keep him. Two years later, they were reunited at a parade honoring animal war heroes. They had such an obvious bond and were so overjoyed to be together once again that Khan's family agreed to give their pet to James as a gift.

The pair returned to Scotland, where Khan spent the rest of his days at the side of his dearest friend.

C. 1936–UNKNOWN
SCOTLAND

(WO)MAN'S BEST FRIEND

KHAN'S family could tell at a glance that their pet shared an incredible bond with his wartime handler. Here are some other well-known hound-and-human friendships:

LORD BYRON'S cherished pet was a Newfoundland named **BOATSWAIN**. When Boatswain died in 1808, the poet wrote "Epitaph to a Dog" in honor of his memory.

JOHN STEINBECK loved his poodle, **CHARLEY**, so much that he wrote *Travels with Charley*, a memoir about their road adventures. John's Irish setter, **TOBY**, ate the first draft of his novel *Of Mice and Men* and he had to totally rewrite it!

PABLO PICASSO was a famous Spanish artist who fell in love with a dachshund, **LUMP**, in the late 1950s. Lump was the only one allowed in Picasso's studio and appeared in fifty-four of his works.

PAUL McCARTNEY bought an Old English sheepdog named **MARTHA** in 1966 that was said to be the inspiration for the Beatles song "Martha My Dear."

MR. FAMOUS was **AUDREY HEPBURN'S** adorable and much-loved Yorkshire terrier. He even appeared with her in a scene in the hit film *Funny Face*.

PINKA was a cocker spaniel who was given to author **VIRGINIA WOOLF** by her friend **VITA SACKVILLE-WEST**. One of Pinka's best tricks was putting out a match after Virginia lit one.

OPRAH WINFREY'S cocker spaniel **SOPHIE** went to work with her and to red-carpet events like the Oscars. When Sophie died, Oprah said, "Nobody on Earth ever loved me like that little dog."

American cartoonist **CHARLES SCHULZ** based his character Snoopy on his family's basset hound, **SPIKE**. The real-life Spike had a bizarre habit of eating razor blades and thumbtacks. Ouch!

SPIKE was the Yorkshire terrier sidekick of famous American comedian **JOAN RIVERS**. He appeared with her on *The Tonight Show* and joined her on the cover of *People* magazine and in a famous advertisement for milk.

ELIZABETH TAYLOR was so besotted with her Maltese, **SUGAR**, she almost refused to accept her Dame Commander title because Sugar wasn't allowed inside Buckingham Palace.

TINKERBELL was a chihuahua owned by socialite **PARIS HILTON**. The purse-sized pooch went missing once and a $5,000 reward was offered for her safe return. She was found six days later.

LAIKA
FIRST CANINE COSMONAUT

After the Soviet Union stunned the world by launching the first human-made object into orbit around Earth, they wanted to do something even bigger—like putting the first living creature into orbit. This was in 1957, when no one knew if it was actually possible to survive space travel.

So it was that a sweet stray dog from the streets of Moscow was recruited for the space program. Scientists named her Laika and she was put through vigorous training for a solo journey onboard *Sputnik 2* (or *Muttnik,* as some journalists called it).

Laika would make history but at a terrible cost. The technology to get a spacecraft back to Earth didn't exist yet, so poor Laika was doomed to go on a one-way mission to outer space. Many people felt this was wrong, and it sparked a big debate about the humane treatment of animals.

The Soviet scientists felt bad about it, too, though they didn't dare say so at the time. One even took Laika home to play with his children—he wanted to do something nice for her as she had so little time left to live. The technicians who put Laika inside her space capsule kissed her nose and sadly wished her bon voyage, knowing she would not survive the flight.

Laika's courage inspired books and films, postage stamps, and pop songs. There's a statue of her at the Cosmonaut Training Center, she's featured on the Monument to the Conquerors of Space in Moscow, and NASA named a Mars landing site after her. Laika was a genuine hero and her memory should never be forgotten.

C. 1954–1957
RUSSIA

SUPERSTARS OF SCIENCE

Countless other dogs have made a contribution to science. Fortunately, not all of them had to give up their own lives to do so, like **LAIKA** did.

After Laika's tragic death, Soviet scientists vowed never to let another dog die in space. Their next canine cosmonauts, **BELKA** and **STRELKA**, became the first animals to survive space flight in 1960 and safely return home.

In 1903, a live **BROWN DOG** was operated on in front of London university students. This practice was completely legal at the time, but many were against it—including Queen Victoria. The surgeon was accused of animal cruelty, and riots broke out when a statue was put up in the unnamed dog's honor. The Brown Dog Affair helped inspire today's animal welfare activists.

Canadian researchers in the early 1920s created lab-made insulin, which is a hormone that people with diabetes can't produce themselves. Before testing it on humans, scientists tested it on ten dogs. One of them, **MARJORIE**, lived for seventy days. This breakthrough won a Nobel Prize, although the lead researcher loved dogs and felt guilty about experimenting on them.

NAKI'O became the first "bionic dog" in 2013. The mixed-breed pup lost all four paws and the tip of his tail to frostbite after he was found abandoned in a puddle of icy water. His state-of-the-art prosthetic limbs made it possible for him to get around and live like a normal dog again.

When Russian physiologist Ivan Pavlov was studying human digestion in the 1890s, he trained his dogs to associate the sound of a bell with food—whenever the bell rang, **PAVLOV'S DOGS** would drool in anticipation. This conditioned response was a major scientific discovery.

Charles Darwin's fox terrier, **POLLY**, went with him on his daily walks and kept him company while he worked. A book Darwin published in 1872 had a drawing of her titled *Small Dog Watching a Cat on a Table*. In many ways, Polly helped make the case for his theory of evolution.

SNUPPY was the world's first cloned dog. Scientists had cloned other animals but never had much luck with a dog until a researcher at Seoul National University (SNU) finally succeeded. Snuppy (SNU + puppy) was named Invention of 2005 by *Time* in the magazine's Most Amazing Inventions issue, although many felt that cloning was wrong—especially with so many dogs waiting to be adopted.

DID YOU KNOW?
ANIMAL TESTING FOR COSMETICS AND MANY OTHER PRODUCTS IS BANNED IN THE UNITED KINGDOM.

MARI
INSPIRATIONAL EARTHQUAKE SURVIVOR

A devastating earthquake shook Japan in 2004, the very same day a Shiba Inu named Mari gave birth to three puppies. Nearly all the houses in her small village, Yamakoshi, collapsed, including the one she lived in.

Mari moved her pups to a safe place, then ran back inside the ruined home to look for her human family. Only the grandfather was there, trapped under a heavy wardrobe. Mari licked his face and gazed into his eyes, rekindling his will to live. The frail and elderly man struggled to free himself, then spent two hours making his way down the stairs. Mari stayed with him, running back and forth between the old man and her newborn pups.

All the villagers had to be evacuated, but there was no room on the helicopters for pets. The grandfather had no choice but to leave Mari behind. Heartbroken, he put out all the food and water he had for her and prayed that she and her babies would be okay on their own for a while.

The villagers were finally allowed to return two weeks later. Mari's family searched and searched until they found her. She was much thinner but proudly stood guard over her roly-poly puppies, protecting and nursing them as best she could among the ruins and rubble. Mari was reunited with the grandfather, who tearfully thanked her for saving his life.

Mari's inspiring story was adapted into a film and a popular children's book. And when the villagers held their annual fireworks celebration the following year, they called it Fireworks for Mari in honor of her bravery and devotion.

BORN C. 2003
JAPAN

THE DOG FROM NOSE TO TAIL

- Dogs have about 1,700 **TASTE BUDS**. Humans have 9,000.

- Dogs have a wider field of vision than humans due to the placement of their **EYES**.

- The **HEARTS** of large dogs beat between 60 and 100 times a minute, small dogs 100 to 140 times.

- A dog's **WHISKERS** are touch-sensitive hairs that can sense changes in air flow.

- Dogs have three **EYELIDS** on each eye, for extra protection.

- Dogs can wiggle each **NOSTRIL** independently.

- Most of a dog's sweat glands are between the pads of its **PAWS**.

- A dog's **NOSE** print is as one-of-a-kind as a human fingerprint.

- Dogs have around eighteen muscles controlling their **EARS**.

- 🐾 Dogs' **EYES** can see better in the dark than human eyes.

- 🐾 A dog's unique scent comes from **GLANDS** around its rear end.

- 🐾 A dog's **SHOULDER BLADES** aren't connected to its skeleton.

- 🐾 **DEWCLAWS** are like the dog version of thumbs and big toes.

- 🐾 No matter their size, all dogs have about **319 BONES** (depending on their tails).

- 🐾 Dogs have wet **NOSES** to absorb scents in the air.

- 🐾 A dog's **EARS** can hear far higher frequencies than human ears.

- 🐾 Dogs' **EYES** see the world in shades of blue and yellow.

- 🐾 A dog's **TONGUE** acts like a little cup when it laps up water.

- 🐾 Dogs don't wag their **TAILS** when they are alone.

- 🐾 Dogs tend to use one **PAW** more than the other.

NIPPER
ADORABLE ADVERTISING ICON

Nipper was a little dog who sold heaps of records and became one of the world's most recognized images. Yet the mixed-breed terrier's story and the painting that made him famous are relatively unknown. Until now.

Nipper's name was inspired by his rather naughty habit of biting people's heels when he was a puppy. He belonged to a scenery designer and lived at a theater in Bristol, England. When the man died, his younger brother—an artist named Francis Barraud—inherited him.

Francis inherited something else, too—recordings of his late brother's voice. When he played them, he noticed how Nipper's ears perked up. The dog's furry face took on a puzzled expression, as if he was trying to figure out where the familiar voice came from. Francis liked the scene so much that he painted a portrait of Nipper listening to a wind-up cylinder phonograph.
He called it *His Master's Voice*.

Francis tried to sell the painting, but there was zero interest in it at first. One person assured him, "Dogs don't listen to phonographs." Someone eventually agreed to buy the painting and the rights to use the image for a hundred-pound note, providing Francis change the phonograph to a newer disc gramophone.

That dog-and-gramophone image went on to make advertising history. It was the foundation for the iconic His Master's Voice trademark used for more than a century by brands such as the Victor and HMV record labels. Nipper led the way for scores of other pooches to sell us everything from soda to tacos to wall paint.

1884–1895
ENGLAND

ODDBALL
AUSSIE PENGUIN PROTECTOR

Middle Island, off southern Australia, is home to a colony of the world's smallest penguins. There used to be hundreds of fairy penguins on the rugged and windswept island, but that was before the foxes discovered them. Not all that long ago, the colony was in danger of being wiped out forever. Then a chicken farmer named Alan "Swampy" Marsh came up with a radical idea.

Swampy had trained Maremma sheepdogs to protect his free-range "chooks" (that's Australian slang for chickens!), and he thought the same methods could help save the little penguins. He volunteered to send one of his best dogs—the rather oddly named Oddball—to stand guard on the island and scare predators away. The townspeople were skeptical but thought it wouldn't hurt to try.

Oddball's arrival definitely made an impact. Once the foxes got a whiff of her scent and heard her barking, they promptly hightailed it elsewhere. The locals no longer found fox paw prints on the beach each morning and the number of penguins stabilized. Project Oddball was a major success!

While Oddball spent only a short time on the island guarding her new penguin friends, her work led to a permanent Maremma program. Ever since Oddball and her four-legged successors came to the island, not a single fairy penguin has been killed by a fox and the colony's population keeps growing and growing.

The program has been such a success that a film, *Oddball*, was made about it and summertime visitors flock to the island for Meet the Maremma tours.

2002–2017
AUSTRALIA

WHY DO DOGS DO THAT?

Dogs often do things that leave us scratching our heads, although they make perfect sense to a dog. **HOW WELL CAN YOU EXPLAIN DOG BEHAVIOR?** Take this short quiz to find out!

1.   WHY DO DOGS EAT GRASS?
A)   To make themselves vomit
B)   To pass the time
C)   No one really knows for sure

2.   WHY DO DOGS TILT THEIR HEADS?
A)   To look cute
B)   To hear better
C)   Both

3.   WHY DO DOGS BARK IN THEIR SLEEP?
A)   They're dreaming
B)   It's a neurological condition
C)   Dogs don't actually do this

4.   WHY DO DOGS EAT POOP?
A)   They lack a certain nutrient
B)   It's instinct
C)   Both

5.   WHY DO DOGS LICK PEOPLE?
A)   It's a form of communication
B)   It's a sign of affection
C)   Dogs love the taste of salt

6.   WHY DO DOGS WAG THEIR TAILS?
A)   To communicate
B)   To cool off
C)   No reason whatsoever

7.   WHY DO DOGS BURY THINGS?
A)   So other dogs can't eat them
B)   To avoid attracting predators
C)   They are bored

TURN TO PAGE 136 TO SEE HOW YOU DID!

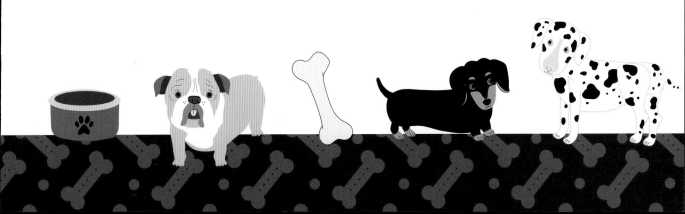

POMPEY
THE PUG WHO SAVED A PRINCE

The Prince of Orange, William I, led the Dutch revolt against their Spanish rulers back in the late 1500s. But the battle for independence might have had a much different outcome had it not been for a silver pug named Pompey.

There came a time during the war when the prince and his troops had made camp for the night. William was sound asleep with Pompey at his side when Spanish assassins crept through the darkness toward the prince's tent. Pompey heard the enemy approach and began barking his tiny head off. William didn't stir, so his dog frantically pawed at his face and jumped on his head to warn him of the intruders.

The prince finally woke up, grabbed Pompey, and had just enough time to mount his horse and escape. He had narrowly avoided being murdered! In gratitude, William honored Pompey's bravery by declaring pugs the official breed of the House of Orange. He also kept Pompey close at hand for the rest of his days, and many of his entourage kept pugs as pets, too.

William's luck ran out some years later when another attempt on his life was successful. It is said that Pompey grieved deeply for his master and died just three days later. An image of the devoted dog was carved on William's tomb inside St. Ursula's church in Delft, South Holland.

Years later, when William's grandson William III and his wife, Mary, became joint rulers over England and Scotland, a number of pugs attended their coronation ceremony, decked out for the occasion in fancy orange velvet collars.

C. 1572–1584
THE NETHERLANDS

RICO
THE ALBERT EINSTEIN OF DOGS

Many people who live with dogs insist that their pets understand what they are saying. Impossible, right? Maybe not as much as you might think.

When rumors first went around about a border collie who knew more than 200 words, folks were dubious, to say the least. German researchers decided to put the dog, Rico, through some tough tests to see if the claim had any truth. What they concluded rocked the scientific world.

In one test, researchers put 200 toys that Rico knew in one room while the dog waited in another room. When asked to retrieve two randomly selected toys, Rico brought back the correct one thirty-seven out of forty times. Another test was even more mind-blowing. A toy Rico had never seen was placed among seven familiar toys. Rico was asked to retrieve the new toy, using a word he'd never heard before.

And guess what? Rico managed to figure out that the new word applied to the new toy. Even more remarkable, he remembered the new word when tested again a whole month later. Language experts found these results absolutely astounding.

Border collies have a reputation for being super smart, but Rico seemed to have a flair for learning that researchers once thought only people had. The question now is this: Was Rico a genius among dogs, or do all dogs have the same potential? Maybe instead of "sit" and "stay" we should be telling dogs to "think" and "innovate."

As Rico was the first to prove, dogs have more going on inside their furry heads than we ever dreamed possible!

1994–2008
GERMANY

HOW MANY DOGS DOES IT TAKE...

...to change a light bulb? Here's a just-for-fun look at how different breeds (including border collies like **RICO**!) might answer this classic question.

🐾 **AUSTRALIAN SHEPHERD:** First, I'll get all the light bulbs rounded up in a little circle...

🐾 **BORDER COLLIE:** No problem, I can do it myself. Then I'll fix any wiring that's not up to scratch.

🐾 **BOXER:** Who cares? I can still play with my squeaky toys in the dark.

🐾 **CHIHUAHUA:** Light bulb? We don't need a stinking light bulb.

🐾 **COCKER SPANIEL:** Why change it? I don't need light to shed all over the furniture.

🐾 **CORGI:** The palace has staff to deal with such things.

DACHSHUND: You know I can't reach that lamp!

GERMAN SHEPHERD: I'll change it as soon as I've rescued everyone trapped in the dark, double-checked that I haven't missed anybody, and secured the perimeter so no one tries to rob us.

GOLDEN RETRIEVER: Don't worry about it, let's go do something FUN.

GREYHOUND: If it isn't moving, who cares?

JACK RUSSELL TERRIER: I'll just pop it in while I'm bouncing off the walls and furniture.

LABRADOR: Oh, me, me!!!!! Pleeeeeeeease let me change the light bulb! Can I? Can I? Huh?

OLD ENGLISH SHEEPDOG: What light bulb? I don't see any light bulb!

POODLE: Let the collie do it. I just did my nails.

ROTTWEILER: Go on, make me.

RIN TIN TIN
HOLLYWOOD HOUND

During World War I, an American soldier named Lee Duncan happened upon a badly damaged dog kennel in a French village. Inside was a German shepherd who had been abandoned with her litter of puppies. Lee brought them back to his unit and found them homes. He kept one of the male pups and named him Rin Tin Tin after a French good luck charm.

Lee took his furry friend to California after the war, convinced that "Rinty" could make it in showbiz. The talented hound got his first big break when he replaced a camera-shy wolf in *The Man from Hell's River*. He nailed his first scene in one take! Later, he starred in *Where the North Begins*, a film so successful that it helped save Warner Bros. Studio from going bust.

Rin Tin Tin made a total of twenty-eight motion pictures, most of which were silent films that made him famous around the world. He received thousands of requests for publicity photos, which he signed with a paw print. At his peak, he earned $2,300 a week.

Rin Tin Tin was so popular that there were whispers he might win Best Actor at the first Academy Awards ceremony. Members of the Academy quickly declared that only human actors would be eligible for the award.

When Rin Tin Tin passed away, radio programs in America were interrupted by a special news bulletin. Newspapers published his obituary, and film audiences watched a newsreel about his life. He was buried in a famous pet cemetery outside Paris, France, and decades later he was honored with a star on the Hollywood Walk of Fame.

1918–1932
FRANCE / UNITED STATES

FILM STARS WITH FUR

Some of the most famous pooches of all time were film and TV stars, just like **RIN TIN TIN**.

BINGO was a purebred otterhound who played Sandy (a mutt!) in the 1982 film *Annie*.

A rough collie named **BLAIR** was the first dog to play a major film role. He starred in a 1905 film, *Rescued by Rover*, which made Rover one of the world's most popular dog names.

BULLET was a German shepherd who starred in *The Roy Rogers Show* on TV. Bullet was a speed demon and was often filmed running beside his costar Trigger (a horse).

Rocky Balboa's "training partner" in *Rocky* was a mastiff named **BUTKUS**. The dog's human companion, Sylvester Stallone, credited Butkus for inspiring the Oscar-winning screenplay.

Dulux paint has used Old English sheepdogs as the brand's mascot since the 1960s. The most famous was **FERNVILLE LORD DIGBY**, who was treated like a celebrity and even had his own chauffeur.

The title role in the 1974 film *Benji* was played by **HIGGINS**, a black-and-tan shelter dog.

MOOSE was a tad too feisty for his first owner to handle, but the Jack Russell Terrier gained fame playing Eddie on the hit TV show *Frasier*. He got more fan mail than his human costars!

The title role in the 1943 film *Lassie Come Home* was supposed to be played by a female rough collie. Yet the acting skills of a stunt dog named **PAL** impressed the filmmakers so much that they reshot all the footage and made him the star instead.

PETRA appeared on the children's program *Blue Peter* and was the first ever television pet.

Former police dog **STRONGHEART** was a German shepherd action hero that graced the silver screen back in the 1920s. He was the first dog to earn above-the-title billing in a film.

A female cairn terrier named **TERRY** played Toto in *The Wizard of Oz*. Terry was paid $125 per week, an astronomical sum back in 1939 and more than most of the human actors earned.

UGGIE is a Jack Russell terrier who stole the show in the movie *The Artist*. He is the first dog to have his paw prints cast in cement outside Grauman's Chinese Theatre in Hollywood.

DID YOU KNOW?
LASSIE, RIN TIN TIN, AND STRONGHEART ARE THE ONLY DOGS WITH STARS ON THE HOLLYWOOD WALK OF FAME!

ROBOT
TREASURE-HUNTING TERRIER

One of the world's greatest cultural treasures might have been undiscovered to this day had it not been for a dog named Robot.

The story begins back in 1940, when four boys and Robot went exploring in the woods of southern France. As they walked along a path, Robot scampered on ahead and started sniffing around a hole created by an uprooted tree. The boys looked at one another, wide-eyed. They'd heard rumors of a secret tunnel that led to hidden treasure. Perhaps Robot had found it!

The boys followed Robot into the hole and crept down a long, narrow shaft. The tunnel did indeed lead to hidden treasure—a cavern completely covered with brightly colored images of larger-than-life animals. They seemed to be moving in the flickering light of the boys' oil lamp.

No one knew it yet, but Robot had discovered what would become known as the Lascaux Cave complex. It contained a stunning collection of prehistoric art that dated back more than 20,000 years. Unlike the simple drawings found in other caves in the region, the Lascaux paintings—featuring a bull, deer, horses, and other creatures—were skillfully drawn with carefully observed details.

In the years to follow, thousands of people flocked to the cave to see the Stone Age art for themselves. The site was closed to the public in the 1960s so the fragile images could be protected from further damage.

What are the odds that a trove of prehistoric paintings of animals should be discovered by an animal? Especially one with such a futuristic name!

C. 1940-UNKNOWN
FRANCE

SALLIE ANN JARRETT
CIVIL WAR MASCOT

Sallie Ann Jarrett was the mascot for a regiment of Union soldiers fighting in the American Civil War. The Union soldiers were fighting for the survival of the United States as well as for the end of slavery.

Sallie Ann arrived at the 11th Pennsylvania Infantry's training camp as a month-old Staffordshire bull terrier puppy. The soldiers named her in honor of a pretty young lady they admired, as well as their leader, Colonel Jarrett.

As the men practiced their drills, Sallie learned right along with them. And when they were battle-ready and headed off to fight, she went with them, proudly taking a position at the front of the line. She even marched in front of President Abraham Lincoln, who had a twinkle in his eye as he doffed his tall stovepipe hat at her.

Whenever the soldiers engaged in combat, Sallie went up to the front lines and barked furiously at the enemy. At the Battle of Gettysburg, she became separated from her regiment during a chaotic retreat. They found her three days later, weak with hunger, loyally keeping watch over her dead and wounded companions.

Just weeks before the war ended, Sallie was slain by a bullet during a battle. Several men from her regiment put aside their weapons and buried her on the spot, even as gunfire exploded all around them. Their beloved friend deserved nothing less than a proper burial.

Sallie Ann had truly been the heart and soul of her regiment. Some years later, when the veterans of the 11th erected a monument on the Gettysburg Battlefield, a life-size bronze statue of Sallie was set in a place of honor.

1861–1865
GETTYSBURG, PA

SERGEANT STUBBY
WORLD WAR I'S TOP DOG

———————————— 🐾 ————————————

When a stray dog with just a knob of a tail wandered into a US Army camp in 1917, no one would have guessed he'd become a future war hero. Yet that's exactly what happened.

The raw recruits of the 102nd Infantry were getting ready to ship out to Europe. Private Robert Conroy befriended the dog and named him Stubby. Dogs were a no-no in the military, but Robert took a risk and smuggled him onboard his troop transport ship. Stubby was soon discovered but charmed senior officers by saluting them with his right paw. By the time the troops reached France, Stubby was their unofficial mascot.

Stubby and his division saw more battles than any other American infantry unit. He once saved lives during a poisonous gas attack, barking and tugging at sleeping soldiers to wake them up. Another time, he chased down an enemy spy and dragged him back to camp by the seat of his pants. That bit of daring earned him a promotion—henceforth, he was known as Sergeant Stubby, the first dog to ever earn US military rank.

By the time the war ended, Stubby was the most famous dog in America. He was welcomed at fancy hotels, appeared at miltary veterans' events, performed in shows, and served as the mascot for Georgetown University. He also inspired the US K-9 Corps, which trained dogs for military service, and even got to meet three presidents.

Stubby gave the American people a war hero to rally behind as they recovered from a devastating global conflict. Not bad for a dog who had a pretty "ruff" start in life!

C. 1917–1926
EUROPE / UNITED STATES

BOWWOW WOW!

SERGEANT STUBBY earned a place in the record books as the most decorated dog in military history. Here are some other history makers:

A Great Dane named **ZEUS** holds the record for being the world's tallest dog, measuring forty-four inches high on all four paws. He was about the same size as a pony and ate thirty pounds of food a day.

The fastest 328-foot dash on a skateboard by a dog is held by an American pooch, **JUMPY**, who did it in just 19.65 seconds.

The record for longest tongue goes to **PUGGY**, a Pekingese with a 4.5-inch-long tongue.

MICK THE MILLER was the first greyhound to run 1,574 feet in under thirty seconds.

A golden retriever, **AUGIE**, held five regulation-sized tennis balls in his mouth in 2003. No other dog has done better since.

TWINKIE, a Jack Russell terrier from California, burst one hundred red balloons by leaping on top of them in 39.08 seconds. That earned him a Guinness World Record in 2016!

The world's oldest dog was an Australian cattle dog, **BLUEY**, who lived to be twenty-nine years and five months.

The largest litter of puppies was from a Neopolitan mastiff named **TIA**, who gave birth to twenty-four pups!

A golden retriever named **CHARLIE** has the loudest yelp ever recorded: 113.1 decibels.

Irish wolfhound **FINNEGAN** is attached to the longest dog tail in the world: 28.46 inches.

SYLVIA was the smallest dog in history. The Yorkie lived in England in the 1940s and weighed just 3.9 ounces.

Before he was finally released, **WORD**, a Lhasa apso in Seattle, spent a record eight years and 190 days on "death row" after two biting incidents.

NORMAN, a French sheepdog, holds a world record for riding a scooter faster than any other dog. He went nearly one hundred feet in 20.77 seconds. He also holds the record for riding the fastest one hundred feet on a bicycle!

A bloodhound named **TIGGER** still holds the record for the longest ears on a dog. His right ear was 13.75 inches long and his left ear was 13.5 inches.

SMOKY
FOUR POUNDS OF COURAGE

After enemy planes bombarded an Allied airfield during World War II, US commanders in the Philippines had a big problem. Telegraph lines had been cut and they needed to run wires through an underground pipe. But the pipe was narrow and seventy feet long. It would be far too risky to have men trying to access it out in the open. What to do?

A soldier named Bill Wynne had an idea. He suggested sending his tiny Yorkshire terrier, Smoky, down the pipe with kite string tied to her collar. The string could then be tied to the wires and pulled back through the pipe. As absurd as it sounded, the plan worked. Smoky was a hero who potentially saved many lives that day.

Smoky later became known for even greater things. When Bill was hospitalized with a fever, his friends brought his pooch in to see him. Smoky did tricks that brought smiles to the faces of the other patients. After Bill recovered, Smoky was invited to perform in other hospitals from Australia to Korea, making her one of the world's first therapy dogs.

Described as "four pounds of courage," Smoky flew twelve combat missions, earned eight battle stars, and survived 150 air raids. A typhoon, too! The fearless Yorkie even jumped out of a tree once, wearing a teeny tiny parachute.

Smoky was honored by the PDSA and also earned the RSPCA Purple Cross, Australia's top award for animal bravery. A life-size bronze sculpture of her inside a war helmet was placed on her gravesite. It's dedicated to: "Smoky, the Yorkie Doodle Dandy."

C. 1943–1957
SOUTH PACIFIC / UNITED STATES

PICK-OF-THE-LITTER BOOKS

SMOKY had several books written about her, and little wonder—her life was like something out of a novel. Here are some other great stories about dogs (some real, some not!).

THE HUNDRED AND ONE DALMATIANS by Dodie Smith tells the tale of fifteen Dalmatian puppies kidnapped by Cruella de Vil. The book was later made into an animated Disney film and a live-action movie.

BEAUTIFUL JOE by Canadian author Margaret Marshall Saunders is told from the dog's point of view. Published in 1894, it's a true story about a dog that was mistreated by his owner. This bestselling book was a major inspiration for the animal welfare movement.

BECAUSE OF WINN-DIXIE by Kate DiCamillo features a lonely young girl and the stray she names Winn-Dixie, a dog that's better at making friends than any human she knows.

THE CALL OF THE WILD by Jack London is a classic tale about a dog that is stolen and shipped to Alaska's frozen Yukon territory, where he must rely on his instincts to survive.

WOOF by Spencer Quinn is narrated by Bowser, who solves mysteries with an amazing sense of smell and his human companion, Birdie.

A DOG'S LIFE by Ann M. Martin is a story about Squirrel and her brother Bone, puppies who must learn to make their own way in the world.

THE INCREDIBLE JOURNEY by Sheila Burnford tells the story of two dogs and a cat trying to make their way home through the Canadian wilderness. The book was the inspiration for the film *Homeward Bound*.

LASSIE COME HOME by Eric Knight is a tearjerker about a young boy whose beloved dog is taken away from him. But Lassie is no ordinary hound, and she walks from Scotland to Yorkshire to get back to her young master.

MARLEY & ME by John Grogan is a heartwarming story about a family and the neurotic (but charming) dog who teaches them what really matters in life.

MY DOG TULIP by J. R. Ackerley is the author's memoir about adopting a German shepherd named Queenie. It was later adapted into an animated film.

OLD YELLER by Fred Gipson was published in 1956 and won the Newbery Medal. The story features a clever, strong, and courageous stray who lives on the wild Texas frontier.

SHILOH by Phyllis Reynolds Naylor is a Newbery Medal–winning novel about a boy who finds a beagle in the hills behind his home. It's love at first sight, and also big trouble.

STATION JIM
VICTORIAN-AGE CHARITY COLLECTOR

Believe it or not, in Victorian times it was no big deal to see a dog in a British train station collecting money for charity. It was a genius idea, as it's pretty hard to say no to an adorable dog. Newspapers printed articles about them and people bought postcards of their favorites.

One of the best-known canine collectors was Station Jim. He was a stray that turned up one day at a railway station in England, a tiny ball of fluff who could fit inside a coat pocket. As soon as he was big enough, he was fitted with a harness that held a small collection box for the Great Western Railway Widows and Orphans Benevolent Fund.

Some dogs were better than others at enticing people to part with their spare change, and Jim was truly a master. He'd wander from one platform to the next performing tricks—he could do things like sit up and beg, bow, shake hands, and stand on his hind legs, much to the delight of passengers.

Once in a while, Jim would hop on a train and roam the aisles all the way to the next station. Anytime someone dropped a coin in his collection box, he would politely thank them with a single bark. *Ruff!*

Station Jim's health wasn't the best, sadly, and he didn't live all that long. Even so, he was so good at his job that he managed to collect a considerable sum. And he is still collecting to this day! His preserved body can be seen in a glass case at Slough train station—if you put some money in the nearby collection box, it will be donated to local charities.

1894–1896
ENGLAND

SWANSEA JACK
FAMOUS WELSH LIFEGUARD

Like many Labrador retrievers, Jack loved water. He spent most of his time on the shores of Swansea Bay and the River Tawe in Wales, keeping a watchful eye on things. One day he heard a twelve-year-old boy call for help and plunged into the river to pull him to safety. No one was around to see it, but the boy told everyone that Jack had saved him from drowning.

A few weeks later, Jack saved another swimmer. This time a crowd of anxious spectators was there to witness the rescue, and his heroic deed was written up in the local newspaper. The town council was so impressed that they rewarded Jack with a fancy silver collar.

Swansea Jack, as the life-saving dog came to be known, went on to save twenty-five more people and two dogs. He patrolled the waterfront, always ready to jump in and help anyone who needed assistance. He had a knack for knowing the best way to tow panic-stricken swimmers back to shore.

Jack became something of a local celebrity and people would line up to pose for photos with him. He was named Bravest Dog of the Year by a London newspaper, and the mayor of London himself presented Jack with a silver cup. He is still the only dog to ever earn two bronze medals from the National Canine Defence League (now known as the Dogs Trust).

When Jack died, the good people of Swansea felt that his many years of selfless service to the community deserved to be recognized and celebrated. He was laid to rest near the sea at a big public ceremony and a memorial stone now marks the site.

1930–1937
WALES

DIGITAL DOGS

If **SWANSEA JACK** was alive today, he'd no doubt have his own social media accounts, like these internet sensations.

JIFFPOM may be the internet's most famous dog, with over 30 million fans on social media. A three-time Guinness World Record holder, in 2017 this cute Pomeranian set a new Instagram record—8.9 million followers and counting!

DENVER THE GUILTY DOG went viral—a video of the yellow Labrador stealing cat treats has had more than 50 million views on YouTube.

A Brussels griffon from New Zealand, **DIGBY VAN WINKLE**, first became famous for his photos on Instagram. Now he doles out advice on all sorts of dog-related topics.

GINNY is a sweet Jack Russell terrier who used to be homeless but is now possibly the happiest dog on the internet—proof of what finding a forever home can mean to a rescue dog.

French bulldog **LENTIL** was born with a cleft palate. After pictures of him went viral, he became an "ambassadog" for the cause and encourages people to treat others with kindness.

MANNIE THE FRENCHIE is "the world's most followed French bulldog." He keeps busy with fan meet-ups across France and helps charitable causes such as rescue organizations and children's charity UNICEF.

MARNIE is a shih tzu rescue dog in New York City who promotes the adoption of older pets. She has a large following on Instagram and lots of celebrity friends like Betty White and Taylor Swift.

MISHKA is a Siberian husky with more than 500 videos on YouTube. Her most popular is one where she says, "I love you." Her rendition of "Jingle Bells" is pretty fab, too.

California's **MINNIE AND MAX** rocketed to fame when their video "The Pug Head Tilt" went viral on YouTube. They've used their internet platform to bring attention to pug rescue organizations.

SCOUT started off life as a neglected and underfed pit bull mix, but later found a loving home and an undiscovered talent—balancing all sorts of things on his head. He even published a book!

SUSIE is the spokesdog of Susie's Senior Dogs. She encourages people to adopt older pooches who have a tougher time finding good homes. Her motto is: Age is a privilege.

TARO AND JIRO
ALONE IN THE ANTARCTIC

Three-year-old brothers Taro and Jiro were the youngest of fifteen sled dogs who accompanied the first Japanese expedition to Antarctica in the 1950s. They were Sakhalin huskies—big and burly with thick coats perfectly suited for super-cold climates.

The first team of researchers planned to stay for some time at the South Pole, but a ferocious storm forced them to evacuate. The dogs were left behind, chained together and given enough food to last a few days until the men could return. That was the plan, at any rate.

Tragically, no one came back for nearly a year. When they finally did, they found seven dogs had perished and six were missing, never to be seen again. Yet to everyone's utter astonishment, two of the dogs—Taro and Jiro—were still, by some miracle, very much alive.

How on earth did they manage to survive eleven months on their own, in such brutal conditions? They had endured winter temperatures that plunged as low as −76°F living on penguins, seabirds, and fish. Equally amazing, they had respected the bodies of their deceased canine comrades.

Taro and Jiro stayed on in Antarctica to pull sleds for the second team of researchers. After Jiro passed away of natural causes, Taro returned to Japan and lived for another ten years. The brothers' incredible survival story spawned books and films that made them national heroes in Japan. Today, there are monuments all across Japan honoring their courage and the sacrifice of the other dogs of Syowa Station.

1954–1960/1970
JAPAN / ANTARCTICA

MUTTS WITH GUTS

TARO AND JIRO beat the odds to survive at the South Pole. Here are nine other dogs who also endured some harrowing times (and lived to bark the tale).

BAN was swept out to sea during the 2011 tsunami in Japan. The mixed-breed dog spent three weeks drifting on a rooftop. The coast guard spotted him a mile offshore and returned him to his overjoyed family.

DEMPSEY was arrested for innocently breaking a law that required "dangerous breeds" to wear a muzzle. Animal rights activists went ballistic, and after a three-year legal battle, the pit bull was finally released from death row.

GASPAR was a dachshund who survived in the Chilean desert for six days. Somehow, his pet carrier broke open on the airport tarmac and he ran off. He was later found, somewhat frazzled and super-hungry, but he made a full recovery.

LUCKY was found frozen to a railway track in Wisconsin in 2005. A police officer managed to pull the husky free just ten minutes before a train hurtled across the track. Close call!

MIRACLE was a German shepherd found seventy-one days after Hurricane Katrina flattened New Orleans, Louisiana, in 2005. She was skin and bones, but food, rest, and plenty of TLC did wonders. She now has a forever home in Canada.

RITA was starving when she was found on the streets in Romania. Kindhearted people put out a Facebook appeal and paid for her veterinary care. Rita survived and her story was a great motivator for local animal rescue teams.

SARBI was an Aussie bomb-detection dog who went missing for more than a year in Afghanistan. An American soldier finally spotted the Labrador retriever in a remote area. She was awarded the RSPCA Purple Cross, Australia's highest award for animal bravery.

SOPHIE TUCKER was an Australian cattle dog lost at sea during a stormy boat trip with her owners. She swam five miles through shark-infested waters to a remote island, where she survived on her own in the wild for four months. A canine Robinson Crusoe!

SUSIE, an eight-week-old pit bull mix, was rescued after being set on fire in North Carolina. Her ordeal led to the passage of Susie's Law in 2010, which allows for tougher punishments for animal abusers. Susie now works to raise awareness about animal cruelty.

TITINA
NORTH POLE PIONEER

In the early 1900s, the very notion of flying an airship over the North Pole was considered foolish, not to mention impossible. Yet Italian explorer Umberto Nobile wasn't put off by people who scoffed. He even planned to take his fox terrier, Titina, along for the ride. He'd found her on the streets of Rome, and they went everywhere together. Even to the top of the world.

Thousands of onlookers cheered as Umberto's lighter-than-air blimp lifted off the ground and floated skyward. Inside, the gondola under the airship was so cramped that his crew of sixteen couldn't sit down, although Titina was quite comfy atop a pile of supplies. The men weren't too thrilled about having a dog onboard, least of all the expedition's commander—the famous polar explorer Roald Amundsen.

Despite all the grumbling, the mission was a success, and Titina and Umberto embarked on a grand world tour. They met with royalty, Hollywood stars, the United States president, and other VIPs, and Umberto insisted that Titina be included in every photo.

Umberto's next polar adventure with Titina turned out to be a disaster. The airship crashed during a storm, and some crew members tragically lost their lives. Umberto was criticized for boarding a rescue plane with Titina, temporarily leaving the other survivors behind.

Umberto spent the rest of his life trying to restore his tarnished reputation. Titina stuck with him through good times and bad, and earned a place in the history books as the first dog to fly over the North Pole.

C. 1925–UNKNOWN
ITALY

TOGO
ALASKA'S GREATEST SLED DOG

In the winter of 1925, some children in Nome, Alaska, had fallen ill with diphtheria, a highly contagious disease that could be fatal if not treated in time. The nearest antitoxin was over a thousand miles away in Anchorage.

A train could transport the serum partway. From there, only sled dogs could go the remaining distance, a journey that normally took a month. Could the dogs get there any faster? It was a long shot but the only hope.

More than twenty mushers and their dogs took part in the life-or-death relay. Leonhard Seppala's team included his best dog, Togo, a twelve-year-old husky who was well past retirement age. He was also fiercely determined, a natural-born leader, and the fastest dog in the state.

At one point during his leg of the relay, Leonhard faced a critical decision—take a shortcut over a frozen but treacherous stretch of water or go around it, which would be safer but take longer. Blinded by snow and battling gale-force winds and subzero temperatures, Leonhard let Togo make the call. The fearless husky led the team across the ice, mere hours before it broke apart.

The precious serum was delivered within a week. Yet, even though Togo had led the longest, fastest, and most dangerous part of the relay, the dog that led the final team into Nome got most of the glory.

To those in the know, Togo was the true hero of the mission that saved so many lives. He went on to become the patriarch of today's Siberian husky line, so his extraordinary legacy lives on.

1913–1929
NOME, AK

HEROIC HOUNDS

Leonhard Seppala described **TOGO** as "fifty pounds of muscle and fighting heart." Here are some other dogs that risked their lives to help people in need:

Labrador retriever **BOSCH** worked for the Philippine Coast Guard. He recovered four bodies after an earthquake and helped rescue teams following a devastating landslide. He was awarded a medal by the president of the Philippines.

BUDDY, a German shepherd, pressed the speed-dial button to call for help when his owner had a seizure. Minutes after he barked into the phone, paramedics arrived, just in the nick of time.

A Navy SEAL dog named **CAIRO** was part of a team in Pakistan that infiltrated the compound of Osama bin Laden, the man behind the 9/11 attacks on New York City. *Time* magazine named Cairo Animal of the Year in 2011.

ELLIE and **JONES** were adopted by a man with type 1 diabetes. One evening while he was out walking them, his blood sugar dropped. He didn't have his insulin kit or his phone and collapsed on the way home. Ellie stayed at his side while Jones ran to fetch the man's family. They were awarded the PDSA Gold Medal for their heroism.

During Hurricane Katrina in 2005, a black Labrador saw a man struggling in raging floodwaters. **KATRINA** pulled him to safety and calmly stayed at his side until rescuers could reach them.

A Doberman pinscher, **KHAN**, saved a toddler from a deadly snake in Australia. The dog saw a king brown snake—one of the world's most venomous—and pushed it away from the little girl. Khan was bitten on the paw but received an antivenom shot and fully recovered.

An elderly blue heeler named **MAX** saved a three-year-old child lost in Queensland, Australia. Despite being deaf and half blind, Max found the girl, kept her warm overnight, and led rescuers to her the next day. Local authorities made him an honorary police dog.

Firefighters battling a house fire in Baltimore, Maryland, found an eight-month-old child inside. **POLO**, the family dog, had shielded her from the flames with his own body, giving up his own life to save her.

WILLIE, a Labrador retriever, saved a six-year-old boy from a vicious wolf attack in Alaska. He fearlessly confronted the wolf and chased it off. The boy was wounded but fully recovered.

TRAKR
GROUND ZERO HERO

Trakr was born and trained in the Czech Republic and later worked as a police dog in Canada. He and his handler, James Symington, teamed up to find missing people, recover illegal goods, and track down bad guys. But Trakr was destined for even greater things.

After the 2001 terrorist attack on the World Trade Center, Trakr and James drove fifteen hours from Halifax to New York City and got straight to work. It wasn't long before Trakr alerted rescuers to signs of life under the rubble. The odds of locating anyone alive at that point were slim to none. But Trakr seemed so certain that they dug down and found the last survivor at Ground Zero.

Trakr worked around the clock for the next two days and nights, stopping only when he finally collapsed from chemical exposure, smoke inhalation, burns, and exhaustion. He was treated and returned home the next day.

In the eyes of the world, Trakr and his handler were heroes. Jane Goodall honored the German shepherd with an Extraordinary Service to Humanity Award, and he was hailed by media around the globe. *Time* magazine even named him one of history's most heroic animals.

When Trakr was getting on in years, he won a contest that proclaimed him the world's most clone-worthy canine. And he eventually was cloned! Trakr would have been super proud of his five lookalike pups, who have all gone on to serve humanity as courageously as their famous father.

1994–2009
CZECH REPUBLIC / CANADA / UNITED STATES

THE K-9S OF 9/11

Immediately following the 9/11 attacks on New York City, about 300 trained dogs like **TRAKR** were on the scene. They searched for survivors and were a great source of comfort during an extremely bleak period in modern history.

APPOLLO was a New York Police Department dog who was onsite within fifteen minutes of the attacks. He nearly lost his life at one point, when he narrowly missed being engulfed by flames and crushed by debris. He survived because he was drenched from falling into a pool of water just beforehand.

BRETAGNE worked at Ground Zero for ten days. She was the last surviving 9/11 search-and-rescue dog and died in 2016. Firefighters and other first responders in her Texas hometown lined the sidewalk and saluted as her body was carried past, draped in an American flag.

COBY and **GUINNESS**, both Labrador retrievers, searched tirelessly through the rubble of the World Trade Center before returning home to Southern California. They worked for eleven days straight in twelve-hour shifts.

SAGE became a search-and-rescue dog when she was only eighteen months old. Her first mission was to search through the rubble of the Pentagon, near Washington, DC, soon after the 9/11 attacks.

Labrador retrievers **SALTY** and **ROSELLE** were working as guide dogs for their blind owners when the planes hit the World Trade Center's Twin Towers. They kept calm as they led the men and their coworkers down more than seventy flights of stairs. Soon after they escaped the towers, the buildings collapsed. They were both awarded the PDSA Dickin Medal for their courage and unwavering devotion to duty in a time of crisis.

SERVUS was a Belgian Malinois police dog from Illinois. He and his handler were working at Ground Zero when they heard three bangs of a fireman's ax on a piece of metal. This was the signal that everyone needed to clear out ASAP. Servus fell twenty feet into a hole filled with glass, twisted metal, and crushed concrete. Rescue workers rushed to his aid and took him to an animal hospital for treatment. As soon as he recovered, Servus insisted on going back to work.

DID YOU KNOW?
THE K-9S OF 9/11 PLAYED TWO ROLES. THEY WERE SEARCH-AND-RESCUE DOGS AS WELL AS THERAPY DOGS, COMFORTING RESCUE WORKERS AND THE FAMILIES OF VICTIMS.

10 WAYS TO HELP HOUNDS IN NEED

No matter your age, there are all sorts of ways to show
puppies and dogs you care!

1. SET AN EXAMPLE. Make sure your dog is spayed or neutered. Sterilization
means fewer homeless dogs living on the streets or in overcrowded
animal shelters.

2. RAISE MONEY FOR SHELTER DOGS. You can do odd jobs such as mowing the
lawn or babysitting, organizing a bake sale, or fundraising for a local charity.

3. VOLUNTEER AT A SHELTER. Whether it's cleaning cages or filling water bowls or
playing with pups, there's a lot you can do to help out. You can even make
signs to hang on cages, like "Adopt me!" or "Take me home today!"

4. ADOPT, DON'T SHOP. There are millions of adorable dogs out there waiting
for a forever home. Adopt a pup from a shelter or animal rescue organization,
not from a breeder. Think first before adopting, though, as it's a big
responsibility.

5. SET UP A DONATION DRIVE. Collect items shelters need, like dog food, toys,
and old blankets.

6. ASK FOR DONATIONS INSTEAD OF GIFTS ON YOUR BIRTHDAY OR SPECIAL OCCASIONS.
Friends and family can donate to a shelter or charity in your name.
Helping dogs in need is the best gift of all.

7. FOSTER A DOG. Many dogs and puppies need a place to stay while they wait to be adopted. It can be hard to say goodbye sometimes, but it's great to know you've helped a dog on its journey to a forever home.

8. BE KIND TO DOGS OF ALL AGES. Puppies tend to get more attention because they are so small and cute and playful. But older dogs are just as awesome, so make it a point to give them some extra love, too.

9. SPREAD THE WORD. Post a photo of a dog that needs a home on social media. Or do a book review or a show-and-tell about something dog related for your classmates.

10. SPEAK UP! If you see a dog in trouble, tell a parent or teacher.

DOG TIP

For more information and other ways to help, check out the list of websites on page 139. You'll find URLs for a number of sites that offer great advice about dog care, inspiring rescue stories, dog facts and stats, dog photos, videos, and much more.

DARING DOGS TIMELINE

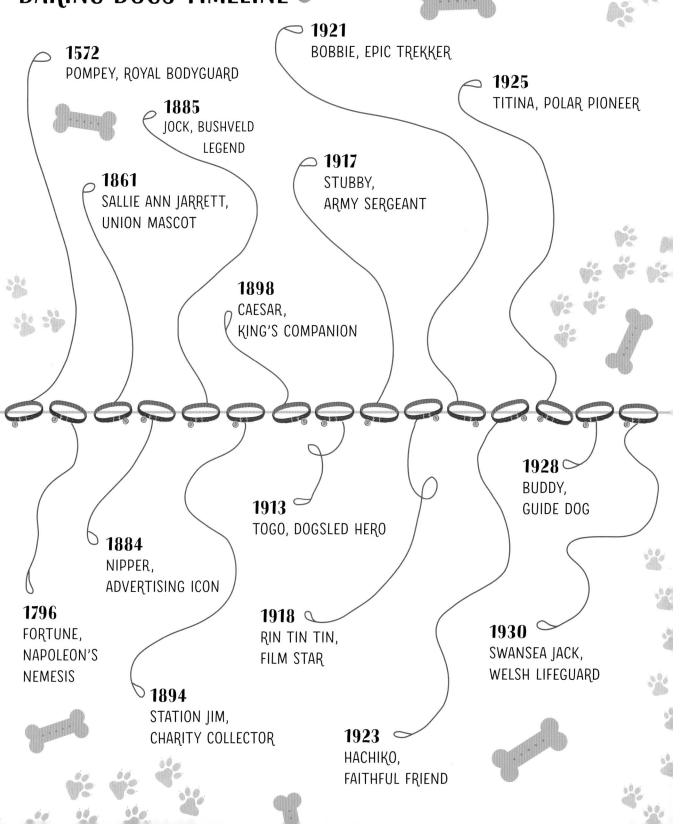

1572
POMPEY, ROYAL BODYGUARD

1921
BOBBIE, EPIC TREKKER

1925
TITINA, POLAR PIONEER

1885
JOCK, BUSHVELD LEGEND

1861
SALLIE ANN JARRETT, UNION MASCOT

1917
STUBBY, ARMY SERGEANT

1898
CAESAR, KING'S COMPANION

1913
TOGO, DOGSLED HERO

1928
BUDDY, GUIDE DOG

1884
NIPPER, ADVERTISING ICON

1796
FORTUNE, NAPOLEON'S NEMESIS

1918
RIN TIN TIN, FILM STAR

1930
SWANSEA JACK, WELSH LIFEGUARD

1894
STATION JIM, CHARITY COLLECTOR

1923
HACHIKO, FAITHFUL FRIEND

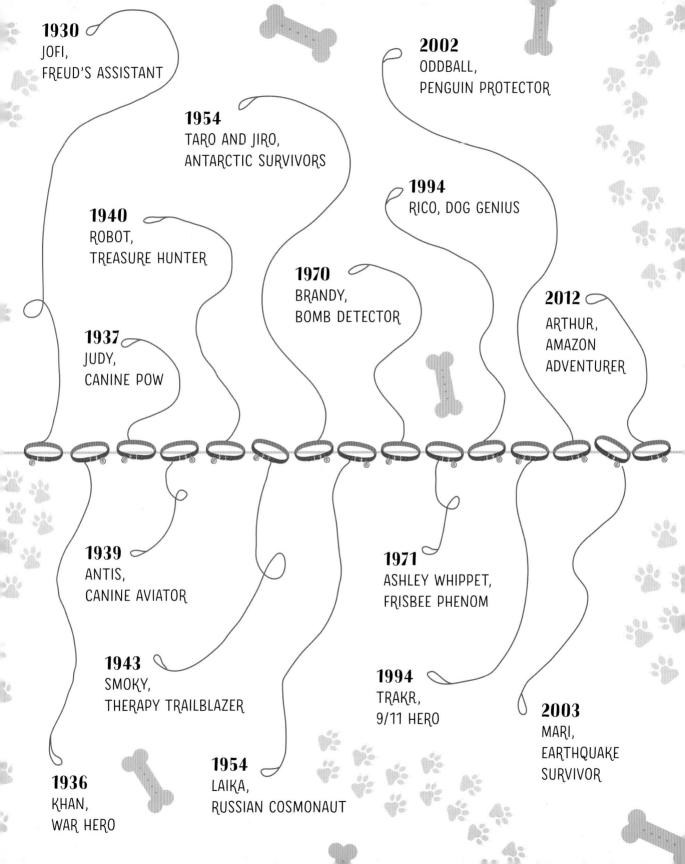

1930
JOFI,
FREUD'S ASSISTANT

2002
ODDBALL,
PENGUIN PROTECTOR

1954
TARO AND JIRO,
ANTARCTIC SURVIVORS

1994
RICO, DOG GENIUS

1940
ROBOT,
TREASURE HUNTER

1970
BRANDY,
BOMB DETECTOR

2012
ARTHUR,
AMAZON
ADVENTURER

1937
JUDY,
CANINE POW

1939
ANTIS,
CANINE AVIATOR

1971
ASHLEY WHIPPET,
FRISBEE PHENOM

1943
SMOKY,
THERAPY TRAILBLAZER

1994
TRAKR,
9/11 HERO

2003
MARI,
EARTHQUAKE
SURVIVOR

1936
KHAN,
WAR HERO

1954
LAIKA,
RUSSIAN COSMONAUT

GLOSSARY

AIR RAID — An attack in which bombs are dropped from an airplane onto a target on the ground.

AIRSHIP — An aircraft that is kept aloft with a gas that is lighter than air, such as helium. Also known as a blimp.

AKA — Short for *also known as*.

ANALOGY — A comparison between one thing and another.

ANIMAL RIGHTS — The belief that animals don't deserve to be exploited or abused.

ANIMAL WELFARE — The health and well-being of animals. Animal welfare advocates believe animals shouldn't be abused in any way or used for experiments or entertainment.

ARISTOCRAT — A member of the ruling class or the nobility.

ASSASSIN — Someone who murders an important person, often for political reasons.

AUSSIE — Slang for *Australian*.

BLITZ — An intense, sudden military attack, short for the German word *blitzkrieg* (lightning war).

BLUE BLOOD — A person of noble birth.

BOMB-DETECTION DOGS (AKA SNIFFER DOGS) — Dogs specially trained to sniff out explosives.

BREED — A specific group of animals with certain characteristics. For example, a dachshund is a breed of dog with a sausage-shaped body and short legs.

BREEDER — Someone who breeds animals, such as purebred dogs. An example of a purebred is a dog whose parents were both golden retrievers.

CANINE — Another word for *dog*.

CIVIL WAR — A war between citizens of the same country.

CLEFT PALATE — A gap or split in the upper lip and/or roof of the mouth.

CLONE — A living thing that is genetically the same as another living thing.

CONDITIONED RESPONSE — A learned response in reaction to a certain stimulus, such as feeling hungry whenever a bell rings.

CONQUISTADOR — A Spanish conqueror of Mexico or South America in the sixteenth century.

COSMONAUT — A Russian astronaut.

DIABETES — A disease that occurs when the body can't use glucose (a type of sugar) normally.

DOFF — To take off or raise one's hat as a sign of respect.

FLEA MAGNET — A dog placed in bed with its owner at night to attract fleas. (Not sure if it worked!)

FRENCH REVOLUTION — An uprising against the monarchy in France, from 1789 to 1799.

FRISBEE — A light plastic disc that one person throws to another (or to a dog!).

GALLANTRY — Another word for *bravery*.

GRAMOPHONE — An old-fashioned type of record player.

HANDLER — A person who trains or has charge of a certain animal.

HAUTE COUTURE — Expensive and fashionable clothing created by a top designer.

HUMAN COMPANION (AKA PET PARENT OR PET GUARDIAN) — A person who looks after a pet animal. These terms are becoming more popular than *owner* or *master*, especially among those concerned with animal welfare and/or animal rights.

HUMANE — To have or show compassion for another living thing.

INFANTRY — Soldiers marching or fighting on foot.

INSULIN — A hormone produced in the pancreas that regulates the amount of glucose (sugar) in the blood. A lack of insulin causes diabetes.

KANJI — A system of Japanese writing using Chinese characters.

KENNEL CLUB — An organization devoted to the breeding, showing, and promotion of certain breeds of dog.

MACHINE-GUN NEST — A hidden place where a machine-gun crew sets up their weapons.

MASTIFF — A large, powerful, short-haired dog.

MENAGERIE — A collection of animals.

MIA — Short for *missing in action*.

MUTT — A dog, especially one that isn't a purebred. Also known as a *mixed breed*.

NATURE BREAK — A polite way to refer to peeing and pooping.

NEWSREEL — A short film about recent news that was played in cinemas before the main feature in the 1950s and '60s.

NAVY SEAL — A member of a special unit of the US military trained to perform missions by sea, air, and land.

NEUTER — Surgery that makes it so a male dog can't father any puppies.

NOBEL PRIZE — Any of six prizes awarded each year for outstanding work in physics, chemistry, physiology or medicine, literature, economics, and promoting peace.

PDSA — An abbreviation for the People's Dispensary for Sick Animals, a British veterinary charity that introduced the Dickin Medal in 1943.

PDSA DICKIN MEDAL — A medal awarded to an animal for bravery during a military conflict.

PDSA GOLD MEDAL — A medal awarded to an animal for non-military bravery.

PHONOGRAPH — An early form of a gramophone that used cylinders or discs to reproduce sound.

PRISONER OF WAR (POW) — A person (or dog, in Judy's case) captured or imprisoned during a time of war.

PROSTHETIC — An artificial body part.

PSYCHOANALYSIS — A form of therapy that aims to treat mental disorders by exploring a person's conscious and unconscious mind.

PUREBRED/PUREBREED — An animal with parents that are both of the same breed.

PURPLE CROSS — A military honor given to a soldier who is wounded in action.

REGIMENT — A unit of an army made up of large groups of soldiers.

RESCUE DOG — A dog that is adopted from an animal shelter or animal welfare organization.

SEARCH-AND-RESCUE DOG — Dogs trained to look for people who are lost or in danger.

SENTRY — To stand guard or control access to a certain place.

SERUM — A liquid that is injected into someone's blood to protect them from a poison or disease.

SERVICE DOG — A dog specially trained to perform tasks to help a person with a disability.

SHELTER — A place that offers temporary housing and protection, such as an animal shelter.

SPAY — Surgery that makes it so a female dog can't have any puppies.

SPOT — Any dog that is seen and reported by players of dogspotting, a game on social media.

STOVEPIPE HAT — A silk hat resembling a top hat, but much taller.

SUFFERFEST — A workout or race in any endurance sport that requires prolonged suffering by anyone who participates.

STRAY — A tame dog with no home or owner.

TELEGRAPH — A communication system for sending long-distance messages along a wire.

THERAPY DOG — A dog trained to provide affection, comfort, and love to people in hospitals, retirement homes, nursing homes, schools, disaster areas, and so forth.

VIP — Short for *very important person*.

WHY DO DOGS DO THAT?
QUIZ ANSWERS

1. WHY DO DOGS EAT GRASS?
C) NO ONE REALLY KNOWS FOR SURE

Only a small number of dogs vomit because of eating grass, plus grass can be rather tasty and gives them something to do. Experts guess that about 79 percent of dogs do it, but why? Truth is, we don't really know for sure.

2. WHY DO DOGS TILT THEIR HEADS?
C) BOTH (TO LOOK CUTE AND TO HEAR BETTER)

Tilting their heads can help dogs pick up sounds coming from different directions. And if humans find that cute and reward them with attention or a treat, they're likely to do it again.

3. WHY DO DOGS BARK IN THEIR SLEEP?
A) THEY'RE DREAMING

Scientists have studied dogs' brainwaves while they sleep and have confirmed they do in fact dream, just like humans.

4. WHY DO DOGS EAT POOP?
C) BOTH (THEY LACK A CERTAIN NUTRIENT AND/OR IT'S INSTINCT)

It could be tidying up to keep predators away or it might be a physical reason, like a lack of vitamin B. But whatever the reason, it's gross!

5. WHY DO DOGS LICK PEOPLE?
A) IT'S A FORM OF CANINE COMMUNICATION

Licking is a huge part of canine communication. They do it to say, "I like you," or "I'm hungry," or simply, "Hey, I'm here!"

6. WHY DO DOGS WAG THEIR TAILS?
A) TO COMMUNICATE

A dog's tail is a fantastic communication tool, if you know how to read it. A wagging tail doesn't necessarily mean a dog is happy — it could also signal distress and aggression. A dog's facial expression and ear position can tell you a lot, too!

7. WHY DO DOGS BURY THINGS?
B) TO AVOID ATTRACTING PREDATORS

For a dog, leaving stuff out in the open is risky—it could attract predators. Even though dogs are now domesticated pets, they still have a natural instinct to dig and bury things.

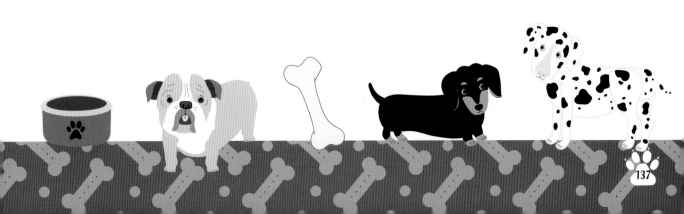

FUR-THER READING

If you want to know more about your favorite Daring Dogs, here are some great books to consider. There's also a handful of doggone good websites on the next page.

BOOKS

ARTHUR: THE DOG WHO CROSSED THE JUNGLE TO FIND A HOME — Mikael Lindnord

BOBBIE THE WONDER DOG — Tricia Brown

BOTHIE THE POLAR DOG — Ranulph and Virginia Fiennes

BUDDY: AMERICA'S FIRST GUIDE DOG — Meish Goldish

ENDAL — Allen Parton and Sandra Parton

FINDING GOBI — Dion Leonard

JOCK OF THE BUSHVELD — Percy FitzPatrick

JUDY — Damien Lewis

LAIKA THE ASTRONAUT — Owen Davey

THE DOG WHO COULD FLY — Damien Lewis

THUNDER DOG — Michael Hingson

TOGO (DOG DIARIES #4) — Kate Klimo

YORKIE DOODLE DANDY — William A. Wynne

WEBSITES

ASPCA.ORG
The official website for the American Society for the Prevention of Cruelty to Animals.

DOGSTER.COM
This site provides all sorts of helpful information for dog lovers.

DOGSTRUST.ORG.UK
This site has a good deal of helpful information and advice. You can also download free issues of their *WAG* magazine.

HUMANESOCIETY.ORG
Official website for the Humane Society.

IHEARTDOGS.COM
This site offers news and information about dogs, as well as fun and unique products that support animal shelters and rescue organizations.

PETFINDER.COM
A comprehensive site for anyone looking to adopt a new furry friend.

RSPCA.ORG.UK, RSPCA.ORG.AU
Official websites for the Royal Society for the Prevention of Cruelty to Animals (UK and Australia).

THEDODO.COM
This popular site has entertaining video stories about dogs and other animals.

VETSTREET.COM
Lots of fantastic information for pet parents, with advice from veterinarians, trainers, and other experts on the best ways to keep pets healthy and happy.

TOP TIP
Always stay safe and be cautious online. Every effort has been taken to ensure the information held on these websites is appropriate at the time of publication, but Scholastic is not responsible for the content on third-party websites.

ABOUT THE AUTHOR

KIMBERLIE HAMILTON used to live in sunny Southern California and now lives in misty Northern Scotland with her fiancé, John, and four cats. She has written all sorts of things over the years, including travel brochures, screenplays, websites, and teaching materials. She is passionate about animals and loves to write entertaining nonfiction books for curious minds. Kimberlie has a master of fine arts degree in screenwriting from the University of California, Los Angeles, and a master of science degree in Creative and Cultural Communication from the University of Aberdeen. She shares her latest adventures and photos in her travel and lifestyle blog, *The Hippie Chick's Guide to the Highlands*.

KIMBERLIEHAMILTON.CO.UK

Also by Kimberlie:
FEARLESS FELINES: 30 TRUE TALES OF COURAGEOUS CATS

Kimberlie wishes to thank her feline companions, Elsa and Whiskers, for keeping a smile on her face during the writing of this book.

ELSA

Purrsonal Assistant

WHISKERS

Mouser-in-Chief

ABOUT THE ILLUSTRATORS

ALLIE RUNNION

Allie is a designer and illustrator. She graduated from the Rhode Island School of Design with a degree in Illustration and English, and has worked for several companies, both on a full-time and freelance basis. Illustrations: **JOFI** and **RICO**.

ANDREW GARDNER

Andrew grew up with four cats and is a lifetime doodler, drawing from childhood. After a decade of working as a designer and art director, he decided to pursue his passion for illustration and storytelling. Illustrations: **TARO & JIRO** and **ANTIS**.

BECKY DAVIES

Becky is a British illustrator currently living and working in the beautiful town of Chepstow, Wales, with her partner. She graduated from the University of Gloucestershire with a First Class BA (Hons) in Illustration. Illustrations: **ASHLEY WHIPPET** and **NIPPER**.

CHARLOTTE ARCHER

Fortunate enough to secure a job with a lovely greeting card company at the age of eighteen, Charlotte become a self-taught illustrator and designer. More than fifteen years on she is delighted to be working as a firmly established, full-time freelance illustrator. Illustrations: various images throughout.

EMMA JAYNE

Emma Jayne is an illustrator from the beautiful county of Cheshire, in the northwest of England. She likes to work both digitally and traditionally, usually starting off by painting with gouache, using ink and colored pencils, then finishing off in Photoshop. Illustrations: **FORTUNE** and **TITINA**.

HOLLY STERLING

Holly is a a freelance children's author and illustrator based in the northeast of England. She loves to work by hand using a variety of different media including watercolor, pencil, and different printing processes. Illustrations: **SMOKY** and **ODDBALL**.

HUI SKIPP

Born and raised in Taiwan, Hui graduated with a Sculpture and Fine Art degree. Hui is passionate about animals, from tiny termites to giant humpback whales dancing in the Pacific Ocean. Illustrations: **ARTHUR** and **STATION JIM**.

JESSICA SMITH

Jess is a graduate from Falmouth University and is currently living in a small town near Oxford, England. She enjoys working conceptually, so scale and perspective play a large role within the images that she makes. Illustrations: **JOCK** and **RIN TIN TIN**.

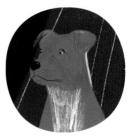

KATIE WILSON

Katie lives and works in an old railway house in the beautiful South Island of New Zealand. She creates for both adults and children, and her illustrations are sweet and cheerful with a handmade feel. Illustrations: **BOBBIE** and **TOGO**.

LILY ROSSITER

Lily is an illustrator, ceramicist, and all-time lover of patterns and picture books. Her work is naive and quirky with a charming, playful twist. Illustrations: **BRANDY** and **SWANSEA JACK**.

MICHELLE HIRD

Michelle is an author, illustrator, and graphic designer. Her work has been showcased on numerous editorial pieces. Michelle was nominated for Best Illustration 2015 Award for an editorial piece she did for *Completely London* magazine. Illustrations: **LAIKA** and **TRAKR**.

NAN LAWSON

Nan is a glasses-wearing, coffee-drinking illustrator based in Los Angeles. There, she lives with her husband, daughter, and two chubby cats. She has had clients in both the publishing world and television industry. Illustrations: **CAESAR** and **SERGEANT STUBBY**.

OLIVIA HOLDEN

Olivia was born and raised in a small village in Lancashire, England. Following her degree, Olivia continues to develop her love for print and illustration, creating her own work for textiles, books, and stationery. Illustrations: **KHAN** and **ROBOT**.

RACHEL ALLSOP

Rachel works from a little studio in her home in Lancashire, England. She finds inspiration in nature and loves to include plants and animals in her illustrations. She spent her early years living in Japan and the culture continues to influence her work today. Colors make her happy—the brighter the better! Illustrations: **HACHIKO** and **MARI**.

RACHEL SANSON

Rachel is an illustrator from the north of England. She graduated from the University of Lincoln with a degree in Illustration after studying for three years in a little studio perched on top of a hill. Illustrations: **JUDY** and **POMPEY**.

BONNIE PANG

Bonnie is an illustrator from Hong Kong. She holds a master's degree in illustration from the Academy of Art University. Her experience includes concept art for animation studios, children's book illustration, commercial illustration, and public art projects. Illustrations: cover.

SAM LOMAN

Sam studied Illustration at the Williem de Kooning Academy in Rotterdam in 2005 and Art and Design at University of Hertfordshire in 2011. She runs her own design business, which includes illustration, graphic design, photography, product design, and writing children's books. Illustrations: **BUDDY** and **SALLIE ANN JARRETT**.

INDEX

FEARLESS FELINES
30 TRUE TALES OF COURAGEOUS CATS

———————————————————⬤———————————————————

Discover secrets, stories, and facts about history's most
fascinating felines! An engaging collection about cats that are the
heroes of their *own* stories, **FEARLESS FELINES** introduces us to
fur-raising facts and adventures from around the world
and across the centuries.

With profiles of over 30 real-life felines, including WWII heroes,
courageous explorers, a Guinness World Record holder, and even
an astrocat that traveled in space (and made it back to Earth
to tell the tale). Plus tons of information on cat activism, feline
myths, and much, much more.